To Lindi
Give t
always ,

NO
MOUNTAIN
TOO HIGH

My Story of God's Amazing Grace

By
PAM EDISON MANN

Romans 12:12

xulon
PRESS

ACKNOWLEDGMENTS

Thank You, Heavenly Father.

You never let go of me or cast me aside. Thank you for loving me when I didn't love you or love myself. You fought for me when I thought I was only worthy of Hell and fought against you. You were always on my side, rooting for me and wooing me to a personal relationship with you. On my Christian journey, I discovered I am worthy of your love only through the Atonement of Jesus Christ on the cross for my sins. I love you, Lord.

Thank you, Ray.

You are my beloved. My life was blessed from the moment we first exchanged emails, and the blessings continue to shower down on me. Thank you for your unconditional and steadfast love. You are all I ever dreamed of and hoped for. God truly gave me my heart's desire. I love you, honey-darlin'.

Thank you, to my children.

Scott, Roxie, Russ, Ron, Dan and Justin. What a gift God gave me in each of you! Scott was my favorite. And then

Roxie came on scene and she was my favorite; but then came Russ, and well, he was absolutely my favorite, until, of course precious Ronnie was born and there was no denying he had to be my favorite. Oh wow, then Danny was born, in the back seat of a car in the hospital parking lot, how could he not become my very favorite! Then Justin arrived and stole my heart away; he was definitely my favorite! What a delight to love you, and to claim you are each my favorite! To be able to feel you are each my favorite shows me how it is possible for us all to be God's favorite. Many times our struggles were great, but it was God Almighty who saw us through those storms. I love you each and every one, the most.

Thank you, to my sister Penny.
There was a short period of time you resided in Redding, and what a joy it was to have you so close! You are not only my sister, you were my mentor. In our frequent sister-to-sister conversations, you would speak of God's good-ness and mercy. I would weep because of how unworthy I felt and while I wished it were true, I didn't think that I was part of His plan. My kids love their Auntie Penny. You are a nurse by profession, and a passionate spiritual adviser by faith. You loved to minister to our medical and spiritual needs. You are filled with a wealth of knowledge and wisdom. We loved asking you medical questions as well as questions about Jesus, God and faith.

During your time in Redding, you took my kids to church every Sunday. They were at the right age for Confirmation and you became their teacher, preparing them, teaching them, making sure they were ready. It was shortly after they received the sacrament of Confirmation that you moved back to the Sacramento area. Looking back, I believe that your being there, at that particular time, was ordained by God for the specific purpose of being the hands and feet of Jesus in our household. I love you, sis.

Thank you, to my brother Jim.

You took care of me when I was a baby, helping mom look after me. You took me in as a troubled teen and did your very best to be a father figure for me, when you were still but a kid yourself at twenty-one with a new wife. I was not easy to live with, nor easy to understand; but you were always there for me. You walked me down the aisle when I married Ken. You were there for me when Ken was killed, stepping in when I needed you most. I still look up to you and admire you for all you stand for. I love you, Jim.

Thank you, Tom and Natalie.

You generously offered me the perfect setting of comfort, beauty and serenity at your summer home on the lake. In the quiet solitude I found it to be the perfect venue to reach deep inside myself and find the words to write my story. I love you both.

Thank you, B.J., Joyce and Shirley.

You are my precious sisters in Christ. Your friendship, love, encouragement, prayers and guidance gave me courage to share my story. God's grace shines through each of you.

I love you, B.J. I love you, Joyce. I love you, Shirley.

ENDORSEMENTS

On these pages Pam has poured out of her heart everything that the Lord has revealed to her to share; her pain, her loneliness, her struggles, her tragedies and her triumphs! So, that those who are going through will know that there is victory! Laced between these pages you can see and hear the voice of strength, power, passion and perseverance. A must READ!

~ Shirley Strawter
Pastor of St. John and St. Mark A.M.E. Church–Plains, GA.

Pam Mann's life story is an example of how God can work in our lives if we'll just let Him in and put our faith and trust in Him. She seeks God always, and in all things. She shares His love through her writing and in countless other ways.

You may meet Pam for the first time in the pages of this book. I have been blessed to know her for some time now and I continue to thank God that her path crossed mine. I love you too, Pam.

~ Diane Pless
Editor, *The Ocilla Star*

Crossing paths with Pam ten years ago began a friendship that has been a real blessing. She is one of those rare jewels you meet and with whom you connect feeling as though you've known her all your life. One immediately becomes aware of the depth of her relationship and commitment to her Lord and Savior and her caring heart for those she meets and serves.

Pam is one of the most disciplined Christians that I know who is seeking His guidance and will for her life daily. Her life is a testimony to this as she has initiated numerous creative ministries to reach out to others in special ways.

Because of Pam's spiritual journey and growth since the tragic loss of her husband and later on her two sons, this book is written from the heart. In it she has shared some of her deepest emotions and thoughts about these times of loss. In retrospect, she understands how God was with her during these times holding her close and carrying her through them. By her enduring spirit, she has grown to be an awesome and inspiring witness for her living Lord. She is a light and beacon of hope to those whose path she crosses. I am truly blessed to call her my friend.

~ Mary Osborn
Retired Educator, United Methodist Minister's Wife

FOREWORD

P am Mann walks with such an anointing of divine favor that I always know she and God – at every moment of the day – are up to something good! He drops nuggets of wisdom in her, and she seems to know exactly when to share them with others.

During evenings of planning for our women's conferences, Pam opens her beautiful home, nourishing us with bowls of hot, delicious, homemade soup. We always go back for more.

In Sunday school she listens intently to the lessons, adding her welcomed insights into the Scriptures. On "girlfriend" retreats, Pam leads all of us into deeper areas of growth by teaching us how to spend quality time in His presence. On out-of-town "girlfriend eating out" trips, she becomes a cut-up and a comedian, bringing us into joyful laughter.

Her victorious Christian journey warms my heart. She has been through so much, and yet her trials have served to bring her closer to Jesus. Pam is authentic. She loves others deeply and serves them with joy. On weekends in the winter, her large front porch becomes a place of refuge for those wanting to have a bowl of her homemade soup. She nourishes passersby. They always go back for more.

When I watch Pam worship, I see a daughter quietly enjoying her Father. During those times, one gets the idea that she has moved away from the cares of this world and into an inner sanctuary with God, a place of complete contentment, as she receives His love and loves Him back.

Pam and I enjoy long talks, antique shopping, relaxing meals, and a lot of laughter. Her friendship nourishes me. As long as she'll let me, I plan to always go back for more.

B.J. Funk
Associate Pastor of Central United Methodist Church, Fitzgerald, Georgia
Author
Speaker at Women's Events
Columnist for the South Georgia Advocate
Columnist for the Good News Magazine

A heart of joy...that's what one finds in Pam Mann, author and my dear friend. It was only a couple of years ago that I had the privilege of meeting this amazing woman. I remember it as clearly as if it were yesterday. I had popped into a local eatery to grab a sandwich when I noticed my friend, BJ, lunching with a lovely lady that I didn't know. BJ introduced us and my first thought was, "How radiant! She's got to be a Christian!" She was friendly, welcoming and pleasant in every sense of the word...and very "polished."

At that time I didn't know Pam's story. I assumed because of her outward appearance, she had lived a "charmed" life, free of troubles. She exuded joy and peace and contentment... and obviously "had it all together." What I would learn about this precious lady in the weeks and months to come would leave me in awe. Never could I have begun to imagine what she had endured along her life's journey. I would learn of heartache and trial, abuse and depression! How could any one person be strong enough to emotionally withstand such depths of heartache? Yet, every time I saw her, I witnessed only love, peace and joy — no bitterness, no resentment...not a smidgen of unforgiveness.

As our friendship rapidly grew, I saw such transparency in Pam that reflected Christ in all areas of her life. Her faith was REAL! In a world filled with "artificial, "fake" and "counterfeit," her genuineness was so refreshing and inspiring. Bits and pieces of her troubled past surfaced in our conversations, but she never expected pity. She shared her story because she wanted to glorify her Lord and Savior, Jesus Christ! That's why she wrote this book!

In the pages to come, you will be uplifted, inspired, challenged and encouraged. Pam's heartfelt desire is that you will be drawn closer to God, our Heavenly Father, as you read her story. As her friend, I, too, am praying for every person that picks up this manuscript. May you be blessed with courage to face your hardships, joy in the midst of trials and that "peace that passes understanding." Indeed, there is ...

"No Mountain Too High!"

Joyce J. Ashley
Author, Speaker and Radio Personality
Founder of JoyJoy Ministries
Books: *JOY JUICE: Delightful Flavors of JOY in the Lord*
      ABUNDANT JOY JUICE, Squeezed from God's Word
Website: www.joyjoyministries.com
Voice of JOY JUICE, a daily radio program
Member of Team RADIATE

DEDICATIONS

I dedicate myself and my work to the glory of God, for it is nothing that I have done, but what He has done in me. It is through faith, by His Grace, I am saved. To Him alone I owe my life on earth and for all eternity.

In memory of Ken, Scott and Ronnie, whose lives left indelible footprints on my heart and in my soul. I have inner peace and a spirit of joy knowing they have reached life's ultimate goal; Eternity with the King of Kings and Lord of Lords, our Savior Jesus Christ. To God be the Glory!

I could not write this story if it were not for the unconditional love of and for my children who walked together with me through our darkest hours, and for whom I struggled to show courage, faith and strength when all I had were tattered remnants of courage, strength, and but a shred of faith.

To my family and friends who lifted me up when I was down, showing me the love of Christ long before I understood what it was to have a personal relationship with Him.

To my precious and loving husband Ray, who brings calmness into my life and keeps me grounded. He is my soul-mate, my rock and my encourager. He is a gifted manager and editor of my work and my number one fan. The Lord did away with logistics and bridged the gap of several thousand miles between the West and East Coasts to bring us together as one; for this no small miracle, I am forever grateful. Ray's ability to love unconditionally is manifest in the person he is. I am truly blessed to love and be loved by him.

PROLOGUE

As I wrote my story, it was very difficult in the sense that I had to look deeply into the kind of person I was, and own up to it. When I tell of my hopelessness and despair, I see clearly now how shallow and selfish I was. I became a victim, in my own mind, of life circumstances from early on, and gave into the notion that I was helpless to change. The more I wrote the more I began to develop distaste for the one I was writing about. That was me! That is who I was! It pains me still to think of all the wasted years I spent in self-pity.

It took disappointment after disappointment and tragedy after tragedy to take me to my knees, time and again, until finally I began to search my heart and soul for truth. By God's grace, that search led to my discovery of the Heavenly Father I never knew, and a personal relationship with Jesus as my Savior and my Redeemer.

Once I was freed from my self-hate and loathing, there was more room for Jesus and less room for old habits. A new and beautiful life opened up to me. I was a new person in Christ, and I would never be the same again.

The following is from
Oswald Chambers
My Utmost for His Highest
November 5th

If you are going to be used by God, He will take you through a multitude of experiences that are not meant for you at all, they are meant to make you useful in His hands, and to enable you to understand what transpires in other souls so that you will never be surprised at what you come across.

TABLE OF CONTENTS

INTRODUCTION

Ecclesiastes 3:1-2, 4 NIV
¹There is a time for everything, and a season for every activity under heaven:
²a time to be born and a time to die....,
⁴a time to weep and a time to laugh, a time to mourn and a time to dance. . .

What would possess a woman to sit down and try to put into words her thoughts about the tragedies in her life? Her troubled childhood–a senseless murder that cruelly left her a widow at twenty-four — the indescribable pain of losing two sons — and to share how she was plunged into the depths of an unspeakable hell? What would be the purpose of such a story as this? Who would want to read it? Who would it help? How could it help? What if it would cause unnecessary heartache and pain for another grieving parent or widow? All those and countless more questions and issues rumbled through my head as I tried to explain to God all the reasons I couldn't or shouldn't attempt to set these memories down on paper.

I feel I have been led to share my grief and my life after grief to you; yes you, the one reading this page this very moment. As I begin to tread the choppy and unforgiving waters in my memory that long ago dared to swallow me up heart and soul, I am reminded that I am not the only one who has suffered unspeakable tragedies. It is only by faith and obedience that I can search the recesses of my memory to begin this journey, led by the Spirit, and set out to accomplish what He has placed on my heart. I don't know all the whys and wherefores; but being obedient to God means I don't need to know. We all have a God-purposed story that He intends for us to share with others; this one is mine.

As I begin unwrapping those distant memories that have been hibernating deep within my soul, thoughts start to tumble out into the words that will fill these pages. Come along with me as I share with you stories of my troubled youth, the loss of my husband and the anguish of losing my two sons. Please, hang with me and don't be dismayed, because the purpose of this book is not to drop-kick you into the sinkhole of my past tragedies; no, not at all! The crux of this story is the hope that you will realize and be witness to a love story in the making; yes, I pray you will see how God's unconditional love, mercy, grace and forgiveness transformed me. As He has done for all His children, He created me for a specific purpose, with plans for joy and enough love to go around all the days of my life.

God the Father, who created me, knew the pain I would suffer in my life long before I ever came to be. As He grieved the death of His Son Jesus Christ, His only child, He also grieved for me. At the time of His Son's suffering and death, His perfect plan was not understood, even by Christ's own disciples. But, to paraphrase Genesis 50:20; *what man had planned for evil, God plans for good.* So, God's plan was the offer of Salvation and Redemption for the world through the blood of Christ that we all might have eternal life — not just a temporary life here on earth, but a perfect Eternal life with Him in Paradise. We will all face death one day, so what we believe on earth and how we live what we believe, matters now and for all eternity.

When we experience the loss of a loved one, grief overwhelms us because we suddenly become painfully aware that we are going to have to live without that person's physical presence in our lives. It attacks the very air we breathe as we begin to gasp between anguishing sobs that never seem to end. Our insides twist themselves into jumbled knots, rendering us a useless, pitiful heap of nothingness.

As by a thief in the night, we are robbed of a cherished piece of our heart, and left with open wounds of raw emotions in its place. Where once the space was filled with love, joy and happiness, tragedy quickly swallows them up and slams the door, and heartache suddenly wraps itself snuggly around emotions of anger, bitterness and guilt. As God would have it according to His plan, we can choose to call on Him for peace and comfort in our darkest of hours. It is then by faith, however slight it may be, we are gradually able to understand and have compassion for those who are also suffering, and the void that once had a foothold is replaced with new understanding. The choice to trust God, when it is beyond our own understanding, is ours alone to make.

It is a lonely journey, being a widow; and even worse to be the parent mourning the loss of a child. It is so tragic to even imagine such a thing that people don't know how to approach one who is grieving, what to say, or how to ease their pain. They might want to turn away when they see you coming, or pass by you with a slight nod and their eyes lowered, fearful of looking into the depths of the sorrow that still lingers in your eyes. Perhaps as you enter a room, the sound of silence becomes deafening and you are reminded once again how pitiful you are.

What a tragic and heartbreaking sight it must have been to see a grieving, pregnant twenty-four-year-old mother of four children, walking behind her husband's casket. He was only twenty-eight. It had just been a few short months earlier that we celebrated our sixth anniversary. Years later I would be taking that walk once again; this time I would be walking behind the casket of Scott, my first-born; he was only twenty-four. Twenty months following Scott's death, I found myself taking the now all-too-familiar journey behind the casket of another of my precious sons; Ronnie was only twenty-two. I never feared nor even gave it thought that I would outlive any of my children; parents are just not supposed to outlive their children. This left me unable to speak of the pain that had taken up residence in my whole being.

How can it be put into words; this lonely journey? I will attempt to do that in the following pages as the Spirit guides me. I began my descent into dark depression in my youth, but the out-of-control spiral downward began June 1st, 1968, with a late night phone call. But first the beginning.

PART 1

Pam Edison

10/27/43 – to – Summer 1961

Also Known as

NEE: Bernice Jeanne Edison

Pam Voorhees

Pam Edison Mann

Chapter One

GROWING UP PAM – THE YOUNGER YEARS

❦

I was born a brat; not just any brat, but a Navy Brat, in Sanford, Florida, on Navy Day. My mother told me that when I was born, the umbilical cord was wrapped tightly around my neck and I was purple and blue and not breathing. Hmm, I wonder now if that is why she always assured me I was not college material.

I was a toddler when my father died in a plane crash, flying with one of his buddies who was a test pilot, the same as he. I have no recollection of him at all. I only knew of him through newspaper articles. I guess it was soon after he died that my mother packed up the four of us kids and moved us out west. She had been crazy in love with my dad even though she suspected he was a philanderer during the war when he was in Europe. My mother would later warn me not to get my heart tangled up with a pilot; but I did and found she was right.

She met my step-dad, Frank, at my grandmother's boarding house. He was the only father I would know. He was neither handsome nor unattractive. He had jet black hair and a ruddy complexion. The oddest thing I remember about him was that after he washed his hair, he put a beanie on his head, fashioned I suppose, out of one of my mother's nylons. I always thought it looked so odd!

He had never been married before he met my mom. He didn't know how to get along with kids at all and I think he bit off more than he bargained for. He was a very strict disciplinarian; very regimented, insisting on complete order. I don't remember my sister ever getting in trouble with him. My brothers, however, had several physical altercations with him over things such as borrowing his socks and underwear without permission. That was always cause for him to erupt uncontrollably. I think they began then to make a game of it to see him lose control. I don't recall him smiling or laughing much. Maybe there wasn't much for him to smile or be happy about.

I thought the spanking that left his handprint on my behind was pretty harsh punishment for my leaving an apple core on his dresser. Now then, when I took a pocket knife to my brother's new penny-loafers out of anger for him not letting me ride his bike, I suppose the whipping my step-dad gave me with his belt was justified.

It seemed he found few things to be happy about, but one thing that did give him much pleasure and feelings of importance was chauffeuring movie stars around when they came to town to shoot movies. Monterey was a popular spot for filming in those days. One of my forever-favorite memories was when Frank took my sister Penny and me to meet Marilyn Monroe at a small, hole-in-the-wall soda fountain in downtown Monterey. He and my mom owned Checker Cab Company and had a limousine service as well. He was the chauffer of many famous stars when they were in town making movies. What embarrassed me was to be dropped off at school in that black Packard limousine with jump-seats. Ugh the horror — we were as poor as everyone else! It was much too showy for me, especially in junior high where image is everything. That was not the image I wanted.

My mother was raised Catholic and we kids were all baptized Catholic. All of us went to church every Sunday — well, everyone except my step-dad. My mother wanted us to start praying for our step-dad's salvation and we did that by attending Novena services at church on Tuesday nights, praying specifically for that purpose. I don't know how long we went, but I do know that eventually he was baptized and began attending Mass with us on Sundays. Our parish priest was a friendly Irishman with a wonderful brogue. He blessed and dedicated our newly built home to the Sacred Heart of Jesus. He became a close friend of our family and even drank a beer on occasion when he came to call. He was always a welcome sight at our home. He wasn't scary like the Monsignor at my church school.

We all called Frank dad, out of respect; but when he left, my brothers and I began referring to him as Frank. Mom and

Frank never argued in front of us kids; so when they filed for divorce, it was a big shock.

I will always consider home to be the little town of Seaside, California, just outside the Fort Ord Army Base to the north, and a few short miles from Monterey, California, to the south. It was there that I went to grammar school. It's where I met my lifelong best friend. It was where I heard the news of my beloved grandfather's death. It was there my mom and step-dad divorced. It's where I lived when the three Hungarian refugees came to stay. I lived there when my oldest brother left to join the Air Force, and I lived there when I was kissed by a boy for the very first time. It was there that a friend's brother showed me how to play a new game called, doctor. It is where I witnessed the house across from our property burn to the ground while a young mother screamed frantically that her baby was still inside. We had lived in that old wooden two-bedroom house just a few months prior, while building our home only a few hundred yards away. The horror of that scene is forever etched in my memory.

Yes, Seaside was my home where I spent all of my tender young innocent years. When I went away to boarding school for my high-school freshman year, I didn't realize that I would never again return to live in the place of my childhood; Seaside would no longer be a place called home.

From very early childhood I suffered with chronic ear infections and earaches which at times caused significant hearing loss. Evening meals at the dinner table were pretty strict when my step-dad was still around. There was no laughing or goofing off; it was all about manners, not a fun time. But in spite of that, and just to lighten the mood a little, without mom or step-dad noticing, my brothers and sister would mouth words like they were talking to me. They would get the biggest kick out of my frustration at not hearing or understanding what they were saying.

The most difficult time I had with hearing loss was at school. Those were the times when a student had to stand to give an answer or to read. When I was called on to read, I would stand and start reading, but I could never hear the teacher tell me "that's enough, you can sit down." Somebody would always have to tug at my skirt to get my attention. So embarrassing! I missed quite a bit of school because I was either at the dentist's office getting teeth filled or pulled or at the doctor's office getting my ears blown out so I could hear. I guess that's when I decided I hated school. From grammar school right on through high school my main objective was to just get through it; and so I did, but just barely.

I did not have a happy fun childhood; that's not to say that there weren't happy times with happy memories along the way, because there were. But there were a few painful bumps in the road also. I struggled and failed to excel in anything; there was always somebody much better, whether it was coloring within the lines or singing in the choir, piano playing or dancing. Well, no, wait a minute — I did win a yo-yo competition in grammar school one time. All through school, my battle with chronic and acute ear infections led to significant hearing loss when I caught a cold. This led me to become self-conscious, shy and somewhat introverted.

After I out grew my adorable tow-headed toddler cuteness and started school, my looks morphed into a tomboyish cartoon character with freckles chasing each other across the bridge of my nose. I wasn't really ugly, but I had definitely lost all my cuteness. My hair was very blond, fine and fly-away thin, and also very straight; my mother had no clue how to fix it to make me look girly. Every few months she took me to the barber shop where she got her hair cut, to have the barber cut mine too. I recall, the poor man used to fuss over me and try to convince me how cute my new hair-do was; but I was having none of it and when I looked in the mirror, all I could do was cry.

I envied my city cousins who had beautiful thick naturally curly hair that my aunt magically wove into luscious bouncy big banana curls. They lived in the big city, San Francisco, and I was a country bumpkin. My Aunt Elynor also sewed beautiful outfits for them. My mother could sing, but she couldn't sew. Instead, she would take me school-clothes shopping once a year, in San Jose; the rest of the year she would give me money to buy clothes at the church rummage sales.

I loved the trips we took to San Francisco to visit with my cousins. My cousin Alice and I are only about four months apart and we formed a very close bond. One particular visit stands out in my mind. I don't remember how old we were, maybe around ten years old, and I say that because we didn't wear bras yet. In fact, we still wore those horizontal-striped t-shirts that everybody our age wore in the fifties. I don't know whose idea it was, but we decided we'd each put two walnut half-shells under our t-shirts. We thought we looked really grown-up and that people would surely notice that we had sprouted breasts just like our big sisters had. So with shoulders back and our chests thrust forward, we proudly strutted our little bumps around the corner to the neighborhood coffee shop. We ordered something to drink, but I don't recall if it was coffee or just a soda. It never occurred to us that we looked pretty hilarious and our sisters had a great laugh at us when we got back home. Those were silly and fun times in my life, visiting my city cousins. The two of us, Alice and I, had to be watched all the time, because we were always cooking up something!

I went to parochial school from kindergarten through eighth grade at San Carlos Catholic grammar school in Monterey. Our teachers were Franciscan nuns who were very old and very strict. Students who arrived at school early were required to attend Mass. Parochial school kids weren't allowed to ride the public school bus back then, so I was dropped off early most mornings by my mom or step-dad on their way to work. As soon as they were out of sight, I would run hide anywhere I could find a place, whether it was under the stairs, behind bushes or trash cans, just anywhere to get out of going to church. Sometimes it worked, but most times it didn't. I am sure the nuns had radar hidden beneath their habits.

During the summer before I turned nine years old, my mother put me on a train to Los Angeles; yes, traveling all by myself! The conductors, I'm sure, were advised to look after me and make sure I got off at the right train station. All my mom had to say was that I was a big girl and there was nothing to be afraid of, and, I believed her. I was going to spend the summer with my step-dad's brother and his wife. They had no children. I don't recall much about them or my adventure except I know I must have been terribly homesick. The woman of the house made a dress for me to wear on my return trip home. It was made of green and white thin-striped cotton with a white organza overlay. They must have treated me special because the one picture of me in my new dress shows that I was all smiles.

I remember a time that my sister saved me from drowning on one of the many camping trips my mom and we four kids took during summer vacations. My sis and I were both on a very large rock that jutted out into a rapidly flowing river, bent over brushing our teeth, when I lost my footing and fell in. She rushed in after me as I was quickly swirling further and further away, holding onto my toothbrush for dear life. Penny was screaming for our brothers to come help, and when she got within arm's reach of me, she grabbed hold of me and shoved me up against a rock, then hung on tightly to me until the boys realized we weren't playing and rushed to pull us out. We were all breathless — Penny and I were crying — as we all ran to tell mom we almost drowned and that I had lost my shoes! My mom very calmly replied that she figured we were all just playing, fighting or yelling like we always did.

Chapter Two

GROWING UP PAM – JUNIOR HIGH SCHOOL YEARS

CRWOℰⅅℰ

A lot happened during my sixth, seventh and eighth grades. My mother and Frank divorced, and immediately there was calm in our home that had been lacking before. But it seemed that was to be short lived, because not long after that, in 1956, at the end of the Hungarian Revolution, my mother took in three male Hungarian refugees that had fled their country. None of them spoke a word of English. My brothers took great delight teaching them all the proper English cuss words; and my mother was horrified. Two of the refugees found jobs and were soon out on their own. Only John lingered around much longer than he should have. He was a short stout man in his late thirties with coal black hair and dark beady eyes. He learned English but spoke with a very heavy accent. I didn't have a good feeling about him. I didn't like that everywhere I went, he was there. He soon began calling my mother "mommy" and sweet talking her. I didn't like that either. There is more to reveal about him later.

A wonderful memory that I cherish was on my twelfth birthday. My mother grew up in Montana and would share stories about her taking off on her horse for hours at a time in the hills and meadows under the vast Montana sky. I could picture myself doing that very same thing and wanted so badly to have a horse of my own. It was, however, an impossible dream. We lived in Seaside; there were no vast Montana skies where we lived; we didn't have the land for a horse, nor the money to rent a stable and care for one. But, on my birthday, my mom gave me the best birthday gift ever; she rented horses for me, my sister and for her and we all went horseback riding for a couple of hours. In that short space of time I felt so special and loved! It was a little piece of heaven; it was the perfect gift.

My oldest brother Jim spent his freshman year of high school at seminary school in Fresno, California. Then, he returned home and finished high school with the same classmates he had in grammar school. The following year, my sister Penny went to a boarding school in Fresno for her freshman year of high school. Penny was always so excited when she came home for holidays and shared how much fun it was. After her freshman year away, she, like my brother Jim, returned home to continue her high school years with the same classmates she had in grammar school. I could hardly wait until it was my turn to go.

My sister was called "Miss goody-two-shoes" by my brothers. The nuns loved her; she was in the choir and sang like an angel; she was popular; she was pure; and she never got into any trouble. My brothers on the other hand, were always in some kind of trouble with the nuns; but even so, they were very popular with the girls. For a short time, they both had the same girlfriend, and that didn't go over well at all. They were both star quarterbacks on their football team. Jim played varsity and Joe played junior varsity at the same time at the same school.

All was as well as could be expected with three teens and a kid sister in the household. My brother Joe lived a bit more on the edge than Jim did, when, as a sophomore, he decided to get a tattoo on his arm. The nuns were beside themselves. His home-room teacher, a nun, told him he needed to go wash it off, "right now!" She didn't believe him when he explained it wouldn't wash it off. He was then told not to come back until it was gone. My mom enrolled him in a public school in Pacific Grove, a cross-town rival. He became their varsity star quarterback. He thrived there, never to return to Junipero. He did, however, maintain all his friendships from his former high school.

All the while, I managed to grow to my maximum height of five feet seven and a half inches by the eighth grade and towered over the tallest boy in class; I probably outweighed him too. I suppose it was because of that, I looked much older than my thirteen years. The uniforms we had to wear were wide-pleated gray skirts that were anything but flattering; white-collared blouses and red cardigan sweaters. That certainly did nothing for my self-conscious, awkward, gangly self. I was not allowed to wear any makeup yet, nor shave my legs or under my arms!

It was also about the eighth grade I began to notice the older boys at the high school across the road; for all the good it did, I might as well have been invisible to them. They were so much cuter than the stunted twerps in my class! The revelation was further hampered by the fact that I had a beautiful sister and an older brother that went to that high school. My brother was a very popular football quarterback, and between him and my brother who was now in high school across town warning their friends that I was off limits, it seemed as though for the rest of my life, they were surely going to thwart any chance I would ever have of falling in love.

Eighth grade was also the same time my best friend and I got hooked on smoking. Unfortunately, it turned out to be a love-hate habit that I alternately embraced or tried to kick over the next forty years. We thought it made us look sophisticated and mature. It was convenient for me to sneak one or two out my mother's opened packs of Camels non-filtered cigarettes that she usually had lying around on the coffee table. It didn't take long before I had a cigar box filled with the pilfered contraband. This was my little secret; I kept that cigar box, with its stolen treasures, under the bed that I shared with my sister.

My sister was the "Martha" in the family and I was not so much the "Mary" but more like, just in the way. She would shoo me outside so she could have the house all to herself. When I was safely out the door, she would crank up the music and start cleaning and polishing, making every-thing shine, as she danced round the house, singing along to the songs of Jeanette MacDonald and Doris Day. She was truly in her element as she whirled around joyfully with her feather duster and broom; dreaming of her prince charming, I'm sure. All that to say, it just never occurred to me that she would clean under our bed! What was I thinking! It wasn't long at all before my secret was discovered. I begged her not to tell mom and she promised she wouldn't, and she didn't. However, she became quite masterful in blackmailing me over the next couple of years, hanging that dreadful secret over my head. If she wanted me to roll up the window in the car, when I preferred it to be down, she would only have to start singing "cigarettes and whiskey and....", that was my cue to get that window cranked up in double time. She says she doesn't recall doing such a horrible thing to me, and said if she did blackmail me, it would have been an awful thing to do. It's okay, sis, I have healed.

Summer vacations between sixth grade and ninth grade were spent in Oregon with my cousins at grandma's house. We had summer jobs picking strawberries to earn money for school clothes. We loved being together. Those were some memorable times. We had to get up before daylight in order to be ready for our ride in the back of an old farm truck out to the strawberry fields. We would pick till noon, stopping only long enough to use the restroom or to eat a snack. We would be brought back home before the heat of the day set in. It took some getting used to; but we were young and resilient, and getting that $4.00 or $5.00 pay at the end of the day made it exciting and worth it. Each night we would spread out our coins on the floor counting and recounting our hard earned wages and feeling so proud of what we accomplished.

Grandma worked nights at the hospital and made pies, cookies, jams and jellies during the day. She had the patience of Job teaching us how to make pie crust (I never caught on) and her famous oatmeal cookies; yum, I can still smell the aroma in her kitchen and taste her cookies. The one thing that she instilled in my young impressionable mind was to "clean as you go." For example, after you beat eggs in a bowl and pour them out, stop and wash the bowl, and if you did that with each bowl, beater, spatula or pan you used, when you finished baking, you would have very little clean up left to do. Thank you, grandma.

I don't think I ever saw her sleep or take a nap; I don't know how she did it, looking after, teaching, loving and nurturing five girls from preteen to teens all summer long. And, just so you know, some of us weren't exactly angels.

Back then it was safe to sleep outside at night in an open yard, or in the house with doors unlocked and windows slung wide open. We spent many warm summer nights sleeping under the stars. There were a few times after grandma got us all tucked in and she left for work, we would wait for enough time to lapse in case she had forgotten something and came back home; then as soon as we thought it was safe, we got up, dressed and off we went to find some fun. We usually ended up at a community dance that was within walking distance. We were careful to be home before grandma.

One particular night, while grandma was at work, I found and drank way too much alcohol. Honestly, I don't remember what the circumstances were, or how I even got my hands on it; I just remember that I was safely back home, in the bed that I shared with my cousin Alice, and I was sick; throw-up sick. My Uncle came to check in on us that one night, of all nights. Alice figured that we were caught red-handed and we would be in a heap of trouble. While she ran out of the bedroom to ward off Uncle Bill with excuses of my being sick, I was trying desperately to hang on to my bed that wouldn't quit spinning. I succeeded in throwing up on myself and then tried to lay real still in my own vomit. Horrible! He didn't believe Alice's story and came into our room and looked in on me. It seemed he stood in the doorway forever and I was praying he wouldn't notice the bed spinning. I am sure he could smell the alcohol and the vomit, but he slowly turned then quickly closed the door behind him. Nothing was ever mentioned about that horrid night.

Grandma didn't receive any schooling past the eighth grade, a fact that was deeply embarrassing to my mother about her own mother. But, what grandma lacked in education, she made up for in wisdom, love and nurturing. She had a way of making each of us feel as if we were her favorite. I loved that feeling of being so special to her! I hope that I am able to continue that kind of relationship with my children, grandchildren and great-grandchildren.

Grandma thought it was important that we keep up our writing and language skills over the summer. A three cent stamp was much less expensive than a call home. So about once a week we would sit down, write home and tell our moms what and how we were doing. My mother never failed to correct my letters in red and send them back to me as a reminder how important it was to have proper grammar. Mom always wanted us to be the very best we could be.

Living in Seaside and going to Catholic school in Monterey meant I didn't have any classmates that lived near me. My best friend Diane lived at least a couple of miles away. I would see her at school and sometimes on a Saturday, if my chores were done. We would agree to meet half way and then walk the rest of the way together. That meant she had to do most of the walking, being more than half-way to my house by the time I finished stalling around with my chores and got out the door.

I thought she had the coolest parents and the cutest brothers; four were older than I and one was younger. I think at one time or another I had a crush on more than a couple of them. I loved going to her house because her mom wouldn't make me eat everything on my plate if I didn't like it. My friend was also allowed to wear make-up and go to Youth Center dances. I was happy about that, because when I was at her house, I was treated like another daughter, and I got to wear make-up and go to the dances without my mom knowing. That would have been about the seventh and eighth grades as I recall. Older boys would ask me to dance and I would be in seventh heaven, feeling quite grown up! That is, until my brothers showed up and let their buddies know I was their sister and not to mess with me because I was just in junior high. That would usually put a damper on the night, but on the other hand, it probably kept me out of a lot of trouble that I was still too naïve to realize I might be getting into.

Chapter Three

GROWING UP PAM – HIGH SCHOOL HELL

I couldn't wait to go to high school — not for the learning but to have as much fun as it seemed my sister and brothers had. Finally, I was through with eighth grade and all that childishness. I was excited about boarding school in Fresno and ready to experience all the fun my sister talked about having her freshman year.

The school was several hours away from home. I wasn't a bit afraid; I was looking forward to this new adventure. As it turns out, San Joaquin Memorial High School was not actually a boarding school. It was a co-ed school with the girls' classrooms on one side of an Olympic-size swimming pool, and the boys' on the other side. The boarding part was actually a two-story house a couple of blocks away, next door to a convent, and run by the Holy Cross order of nuns. The house mother was called Mother Superior and the other nuns were called Sisters.

The boarding house had a large dormitory upstairs that I would call my home for the next year. I was assigned one of several single beds that were lined up on both sides of the room. Our hanging clothes were sparse and we all shared a large closet. I believe there were about ten of us altogether. Just a night stand separated our beds. There were lots of house rules: mandatory study time before dinner; lights out at 10:00 p.m.; no snacks in our room and no sharing or swapping beds. Oh, and no smoking. I also had to obey my mother's rule; no dating until I was sixteen. Well, I would only be fifteen when I returned home, so there was never any chance that I would be able to date while I was away.

I was lucky enough, however, to get to go to the school dances. And wouldn't you know it, I fell for a handsome high school junior, a six foot four jock, at the very first dance. He flirted and then danced with me the whole night, walked me home and asked if I would like to go out to a movie sometime. Let's just say, it was a heart crushing and very short-lived romance once I said I wasn't allowed to date. I had a crush on him the whole school year. It broke my heart to see him with different girls all the time instead of with me.

There were three girls at the boarding house that I will never forget. Even though I have forgotten the names of two of them, I remember that one was a Novice (one who has entered a religious order but not taken her final vows), and she ate with us and hung out at the boarding house from time to time, but she slept and was schooled at the convent. She and I had one thing in common: we both smoked.

When all the other girls had gone home one quiet and ordinary weekend, she and I decided to sneak up to my dorm bathroom and have a quick smoke. The upstairs was normally off limits during the day. We arrived at our destination without being noticed; it would only take a minute. She was sitting on the commode, puffing away and I, barefoot, was standing near the bathtub when there was a knock on the door. Busted! The Novice quickly flushed her cigarette down the toilet and hollered out, "Just a minute!" I had panicked and threw my cigarette in the bathtub to put it out by stomping it with my barefoot, then tossing it in the waste can. All the while the Sister was demanding we open the door. The Novice looked at me pleading that I not tell on her or she would be kicked out of the Convent. I promised.

When I opened the door, the smoke wafted out into the room past the Sister's nose. She asked if I had been smoking; I couldn't very well deny it. I confessed. She wanted to know why I was in the bathroom with the Novice; I had no answer without implicating my friend. Sister asked me if my mother knew I smoked and I said no. She then grounded me and ordered me to write a letter to my mother telling her I had been disobedient. The Novice was never questioned. And soon after that, I never saw her again. I never did write that letter to my mother.

I was allowed to babysit sometimes and sometimes I said I was babysitting when I was actually out with friends from school. I got away with it; it was one thing I did and never got caught. Other than smoking and lying about where I was going, it was all pretty innocent by today's standards.

I didn't get to go home on weekends; just Thanksgiving, Christmas and Easter. So, my first trip home was for Thanksgiving. The day before Thanksgiving, I got myself to the Greyhound Bus Depot in Fresno, bought a ticket to Monterey, hopped aboard the bus and was excited to be going home. I had just turned fifteen the month before and I was feeling pretty grown-up. In about five or six hours I would be home! I fell asleep shortly after the bus pulled out and when I awoke it was dark. I asked the man next to me how much longer he thought it would be until we reached Monterey. He gave me a funny look and said the bus was headed to Los Angeles. Los Angeles? But I needed to go to Monterey. The man told the bus driver and the driver notified the station in Los Angeles that he had a passenger that was on the wrong bus. In the meantime, my mother had contacted the California Highway Patrol and the Sheriffs' Departments up and down the state, checked all the hospitals between Fresno and Monterey, looking for me. She contacted my Aunt, who at the time worked for the San Francisco Juvenile Department, and her comment to my mother was that I possibly ran away with a boyfriend. My mother was frantic; and so was I. As we pulled into the station in Los Angeles the bus driver got a ticket for me to get on the next bus heading back to Monterey and gave me $5.00 to get something to eat.

I arrived in Monterey the next day about noon. When I got off the bus, I went to the nearest payphone and called home. My mother cried when she heard my voice. Nobody, including me, had called her to tell her of my misfortune of getting on the wrong bus; she thought I must have been kidnapped. I guarantee you, heads rolled at Greyhound corporate offices. It was a joyful weekend once we all caught up on our lost sleep, and then too soon it was time to hop on a bus and head back to the boarding house and school. I learned the hard way to check for myself which bus I needed to board.

I don't recall exactly what time of year it was, perhaps a little before Easter vacation, when all the girls from the boarding house went home except for a Porterville, California girl and me. She and I had become good friends and we decided we were going to bend the rules just a bit, since it was just the two of us. We loaded up on snacks and Cokes® and then snuck our contraband upstairs in our dorm for our midnight snack. During the week, the house Mother Superior slept in the adjoining room, but on weekends when there were only one (me) or two of us, she slept down the hall. That was perfect for what we had planned.

We were so excited for lights out at 10:00 p.m. We waited for a few minutes, and then my friend got what she had hidden under her bed and brought it over to my bed and stuck it under the covers. I gathered up what I had and added it to the pile under the covers. Oh gosh, what a treat! We could hardly contain ourselves. I had a little flashlight and we both pulled the covers over our heads and dug into the goodies, trying to be quiet but giggling about what we were getting away with. All of a sudden, the door to the dorm crashed open and there stood the Mother Superior in her high-necked, full-length, long-sleeved white cotton nightgown, and wearing a little white cotton bonnet which completely covered her head. She was scowling at us as she flipped on the light. We had quickly come out of our tent of blankets and held them up under our chins attempting to hide the bounty underneath and trying not to giggle, thinking we were going to get away with it.

Oh, but not so. It was much more serious than what we ever could have imagined. I was taken downstairs into the Mother Superior's office where I was confronted by two very angry Sisters. I didn't understand why they were so angry — they didn't even see all the food we had hidden! One nun looked at me and said, "I have called your mother and she will be here in the morning and we shall have a talk then." I wondered out loud why in the world they would call my mother, and I remember hearing one saying that they believed I was a homosexual. I had never heard that word before, but by the tone of their voice I knew it must be something pretty bad.

When my mother arrived the next morning, she hugged me and assured me everything would be all right. The Mother Superior spoke with her privately. Then when we were all together they asked me what my friend and I were doing in my bed. I confessed about breaking the rules of having food in the dorm, and about putting all the food under the covers on my bed, and my friend and I hiding under the covers giggling about how we were getting away with eating all the goodies and not getting caught. Then I told them I didn't know what homosexual meant. It was never explained to me, ever; not by the nuns then, nor by my mother later.

They agreed to let me stay and finish the school year, but I would be punished for breaking the rules and have to move downstairs, away from the rest of the girls. I would be a roommate to a paraplegic girl that was two years my senior. It would be my job to help her in and out of bed and in and out her wheelchair. It became my job to help her with anything she wasn't able to do herself and wheel her to and from school in her wheelchair. All I will say about her is that she became quite demanding and wasn't very friendly at all.

I felt this punishment was pretty extreme for the crime I committed of having food upstairs in my bed. I don't believe they gave my friend and partner-in-crime punishment for her part. Our friendship waned as I basically was out of touch with the girls who lived in the dorm upstairs. I was no longer one of them, but instead a servant to the handicapped girl downstairs. I hated school and being at the boarding house. I was so lonely, especially on weekends when everybody went home! Why did the nuns love my sister so much, but hate me? Why was I an outcast? I longed to be home with my family and my hometown school friends and my best friend.

By the time the school year was out, my oldest brother Jim was still away in the Air Force, my sister Penny was in her second year of nursing school, my brother Joe was living on his own going to college, and my mother had accepted a job in San Francisco, sold our home and moved into a studio apartment in downtown San Francisco.

Finally, I would be going home – not to the home I left, not to the home I knew, but wherever my mom was; that would be home to me. It wasn't exactly what I expected, although I'm not exactly sure what it was I did expect. The apartment was a little one-room studio apartment smack dab in the middle of downtown San Francisco; most probably, I would guess, from the 1940's era; quaint, compact and cozy, for sure. My mother and I shared a rollaway bed and although the apartment was cramped, I enjoyed being with her again; I would have her all to myself. It had been a very long time since I was "home;" and for a time, it felt so good to be away from the scrutiny of the Holy Cross nuns that ran the boarding house and taught at the high school. Unfortunately, real life got in the way of this young girl's fairytale, and cold reality crashed my fantasy of daydreaming and watching clouds change magically into whatever my imagination could see. It was time for me to get enrolled in a new school. Of course, it had to be the largest high school in San Francisco. George Washington High School was a public school with approximately 2,000 students. That in itself was overwhelming to me. I was lost in a sea of strangers as I tried to find my way around an enormous campus.

I felt like an alien in class because it was my first exposure to public school where the kids didn't bother to stand when an adult entered, and they didn't stand to answer questions. I made the mistake of standing when no one else

55

did, because it embarrassed me not to. But it didn't take long before I got in the groove of just staying seated and feeling less embarrassed. I hated feeling like that; I wasn't brought up to be rude, and to me, this was just plain rude. Yet, I didn't want to be the odd one out either; I just wanted to blend in with my classmates and be kind of invisible.

I was rather plain looking, I thought. I didn't wear any make-up except mascara. One day out of the blue, a boy approached me and made a suggestion that I would be more attractive if I used some eye make-up. I thought it both odd and awkward. When I got home I took a long look in the mirror and then decided to take him up on that suggestion, figuring I didn't have anything to lose. The only make-up I had ever worn was lipstick and mascara. I was lazy; I thought that was enough. It turned out that all I needed to attract attention and make a few friends was just a little make-up and suddenly I was somebody else!

The school was way out near the beach and we lived downtown; I would have to ride public transportation, and make a transfer to a second bus to get to my school. During one of my many bus rides to school, I met a young black guy, a junior at George Washington High School. Honestly, I can't recall his real name because I always called him Johnny. He started sitting next to me and would make small talk and then one morning on the way to school, he began singing to me! He sounded "exactly" like Johnny Mathis! I loved his voice and I loved for him to sing to me. I gave him my number and he would call me and sing to me. One day he asked me if I wanted to go to the movies with him and some friends. I asked my mom, since I had not ever been allowed to date yet. Because it wasn't actually a date alone with someone, she agreed that I could go. She had only one bit of advice, since I was still pretty naïve. She said that some people wouldn't like the fact that I was a white girl going out with a guy that was black, and that they might say mean things to us that would hurt my feelings or make me mad, and that I would just have to have thick skin if I wanted to go out with him. He and I had a fun time but I wasn't mature enough to ignore the stares we got and that made me uncomfortable. Our friendship remained, and he continued to call me and sing to me, but we didn't venture out on anymore dates.

It seemed like forever, but it was actually only a couple of months after school started when my mother found a two-bedroom apartment just down a steep hill from the high school and right across the street from Golden Gate Park. That meant I could walk to school, and she would have to ride buses to work. That worked out great for me! Unfortunately, I wasn't thinking about the inconvenience to her. I wouldn't have to stay at school for lunch and feel lost in a sea of kids I didn't know. I still felt so out of place! They all looked as if they were having a great time.

I was missing my friends in Monterey; my sister was still attending nursing school in San Francisco and living on campus and I missed her terribly; my mom was gone in the morning when I left for school and came home late in the evening, exhausted. I was lonely, just as if I were back at the boarding house. On weekends I would sometimes get to spend time with my cousin Alice, who lived on the other side of Golden Gate Park. It seemed like every time we got together, what one didn't think up, the other one did. Mischief seemed to follow us around, just waiting for us to discover it. We did some pretty stupid things and only God's hands on our lives kept us safe. We didn't break any laws or do anything to harm anyone and we weren't really bad, but we took a lot of unnecessary chances walking alone through Golden Gate Park; picking up strangers at the boardwalk and then fibbing to my mom where we met them. We thought we were pretty grown up, but actually we were still very naïve and, very lucky.

Christmastime, when I was fifteen and Alice was fourteen, found us being shipped off to grandma's house in Oregon. We were to be in charge of Alice's little brothers — Steve who was about ten and Bobbie, six, and little sister Mary who was about five. Actually, we loved being at grandma's house and all too soon it was time to go home. It was especially difficult for me because I had met a boy named Gene; I thought he was eighteen and he thought I was eighteen. He was an artist and he drove an MG sporty car that had no top. I was crazy about him and he was crazy about me. He was sweet and very much a gentleman. I discovered later that he was actually twenty-four. I was just fifteen. He promised he would write to me after I went back home and he would wait for me until I was eighteen.

Alice and I would be taking a train ride home from Portland, Oregon to San Francisco and she and I were to be in-charge of her siblings, Steve, Bobby and Mary. Oh my goodness, can you imagine putting a fifteen- and a four-teen-year-old in charge of a ten-, a six- and a four-year-old on a twelve-hour train ride? Not a problem. Alice and I had it all figured out. We bought a carton of Marlboro cigarettes; we wanted to make sure we would have enough for the trip; then we got the two youngest, Bobby and Mary, all snuggled in their seats and told Steve to keep an eye on them, and that we would be upstairs in the dome of the train if he needed us. With that all nicely taken care of, we proceeded up to the dome where we could look out the windows all around, and sit and smoke like we were oh, so grown-up! I remember the scenery was breathtaking with blankets of snow covering everything in sight. It was like a winter wonderland. It looked so peaceful and beautiful.

The sad part of the trip was as we passed through Clackamas, the train would be going right past my boyfriend Gene's house. And there he was, sitting on the rooftop of his home, waving goodbye to me, as the train rolled on by. I am sure he didn't see me frantically waving back. I soon grew tired of riding on that train, of smoking and looking out the windows and every now and then having to check on Steve. Being all grown up just wasn't all that it was cracked up to be! Thank goodness I had Alice to lighten my mood; we were in this together. We made Steve take a puff of a cigarette so he wouldn't tell on us.

Many long hours later, as we rolled into the San Francisco train station, Alice and I retrieved the three kids. I thought it miraculous that they came through the long train ride unscathed. Nobody would be the wiser that we had not hovered over them the whole time. All that in check, we still had nine packs of cigarettes to dispose of, so we frantically began handing them out to strangers, trying to get rid of the contraband before we got off the train. Strangers were happy to oblige us. A carton of cigarettes; what were we thinking? It's hilarious now, looking back as I recall that day; we must have looked like cartoon caricatures instead of what we thought was looking grown-up. God must have truly been watching over the three of us, shaking His head for sure.

My cousin and I graduated from those teeny-bop antics, to what we thought was the big time. Alice, her older sister Beverly and sometimes her sister Donna, and I, would tell our moms we were going downtown to the movies. Well, we did go downtown, but instead of going to the movies, we took a jitney to Hunters Point Naval Shipyard, and there we danced the night away at the Enlisted Men's Club where there were at least a hundred available young men in uniform. It was one of the very safest places we could go because the guys were so respectful and just plain lonely. The age requirement was eighteen to be allowed in, because alcohol was served. We looked every bit of eighteen and there were no questions asked as we strolled in the club with confidence. At fifteen, I looked every bit of eighteen and felt so grown up!

We added a little drinking to our fun night out because on a military base the drinking age was lowered from twenty-one to eighteen. We thought we were having the best times of our lives and getting away with it. But being so deceitful to my mother was beginning to wear on me, because one lie would lead to another, then another and another. It was becoming difficult to keep them straight.

While I enjoyed the fun, excitement and all the flattery and attention I received, it all became so shallow without depth or meaning. My life was truly an empty shell, empty inside, and without purpose, something was missing; I had not a clue what it was. My actions were becoming more and more out of control. I wasn't raised in the streets but I began acting as if I had been; as if I had no better upbringing. I was living dangerously and flirting with the unknown. I smoked because I thought it made me <u>look</u> grown-up; and then it became a habit. I drank to <u>feel</u> grown-up and to fit in, even though I didn't like the taste of it.

I felt as if I were a loose cannon, out of control and on a path to self-destruction. What was missing in my life that I couldn't be content? I had been brought up with strict boundaries, and now, with little direction, I had more freedom to make my own decisions. I didn't like the person I was afraid I was becoming. Where was I going in life, what were my plans for my future? I was sure my mother loved me, but I began to feel I was an inconvenience to her. She had low expectations of me; I was never encouraged to feel I could become successful in anything important. Deep down I was angry and resentful that I did not get to continue my education with my friends I grew up with in Monterey. I spent a lot of time feeling sorry for myself.

One night my sister came to see us. While she was in the other room talking with my mom, I got this overwhelming feeling of hopelessness. I was unhappy, depressed and feeling sorry for myself. I missed my sister; I missed my life when we were all a family. My life was not worth living; I had nothing to work towards, nothing to look forward to, and no dreams of a brighter future. My going out and being wild and living on the edge left me empty. I didn't know what I wanted and didn't know what I was looking for; I just knew I didn't want my life to continue as it was. I locked myself in the bathroom and opened the medicine cabinet and whatever medication was in there, I took it all; and I waited.

Did I actually want to end my life? No, not forever, just for a little while until it became something better. It was pretty quickly that I began to get really sick and it scared me. I called out to my sister and when she saw me, she knew something was dreadfully wrong. I told her what I had done and begged her to promise not to tell mom. She couldn't make that promise. She was studying to become an RN, and she knew I was in serious trouble.

I don't remember how I got to the county hospital and I only vaguely remember them pumping my stomach; afterwards, I was put in a small dark padded cell with a bare light bulb hanging high up from the ceiling. I was there long enough for them to figure out what they could do with me. My sister tells me that when they let her come see me in that cell, I was curled up in a fetal position and not speaking. I don't remember that and I don't know how long I was in that padded cell all alone. Did I know God was with me? No, I didn't. In hindsight, I know that He was indeed right there with me.

As I look back at this pitiful fifteen-year-old lost, lonely and hopeless child, completely alone in an honest-to-goodness dimly lit padded cell, I weep for her because she had no idea how much she was loved by her family, and that God loved her and had plans for her. It pains me so to relive this memory of her; that part of me. The next thing I remember is a huge dim room filled with rows of beds; probably fifteen or twenty of them. The nurses had taken from me all my personal belongings. I was given a gown to wear and I was taught to curl my hair with rags because I couldn't have any sharp objects; that meant no pens, pencils, no razor to shave my legs, nothing. I was shown to my bed, and as I looked around I saw that there were no young people in this room; they were in various stages of "old" to "ancient." Some of them held baby dolls, some were looking for their children under pillows and some just sat up in their beds and spoke to invisible people. So this is where crazy people go; this is what I am, crazy. In the day time the ladies and I would go sit out on the veranda and stare at one another; sometimes they would engage me in conversation; usually about how young I was and what on earth brought me there. They took a liking to me and gave me the nickname "Peanut." I liked that and I liked the attention they gave me.

When the doctors came on their rounds, there were about three or four of them all bunched at the foot of my bed, and they would ask me if I was ready to go home. My answer was always, "No." Nothing had changed in my life; why would I want to go back home? I felt safe and secure here; I didn't have to measure up or meet anyone's expectations. The rules were easy enough to keep so I didn't worry about breaking them or disappointing anyone. I could just stay there indefinitely and that would suit me fine. In fact, the first few times my mother came to visit, I said I didn't want to see her. I don't know why I did that to her. I put her through hell because I didn't know how to cope.

Like a spoiled child and a fragile egg all rolled up in one, I agreed to go home if I could smoke in front of my mother and if I could see my boyfriend that lived in Oregon. Both requests were honored, and I finally went home. They sent for Gene from Oregon and he came and stayed with us for a couple of weeks. He still cared a lot about me as I did him. There were many opportunities he had to take advantage of me and to his credit and honor he didn't even try. What he did do was answer all my questions and explain as delicately as possible all my questions about sex that I could think to ask him. My mother never found the right time to tell me about the birds and the bees; and that was a time when such things weren't taught in school.

In his presence, and to his credit, Gene was able to make me feel like a delicate and beautiful flower that he cherished. When he finally had to leave, he promised me he would write to me every week; he never did and then I became convinced that he was just another shallow relationship. It was decades later I found out from my sister, that he had written to me and my mother intercepted all the letters that he wrote until after a while, they stopped coming.

Some counseling and Rorschach tests were in order after my release from the hospital and then I would be good as new. I think one of the things discovered in therapy was that I missed having a family life. Being the last one at home, holidays didn't have the same excitement and weren't as important. My step-dad and mom even went to therapy together for my sake, to see if they could be civil enough to each other so that the three of us could do things together. The thought was a good one but in reality it wasn't such a good idea. But, I have to give them credit; they did give it a try.

The ink blot tests were fun and brought out the creativity in me I didn't know I had. I messed up describing one ink-blot they showed me, by saying it looked to me like a girl was jumping off a bridge. That's what came out of my mouth, but not what I meant to say. I meant to say it looked as if she was "walking" across the bridge; she was clearly not jumping! They wouldn't let me correct it and because of that one gaff, I overheard the therapist tell my mother, clearly as if I wasn't in the room, that I had suicidal tendencies and would probably attempt it again and again. So, that was my destiny, I thought to myself, as I quickly stuffed the words deep in my subconscious trying desperately to "*un*-hear" what I had just heard.

Mom understood I was an unhappy child and that I needed supervision. Her working hours did not allow time for that, and I obviously wasn't stable enough or mature enough to be left so many hours on my own. She made arrangements with my oldest brother Jim and my sister-in-law Teri for me to come live with them in Riverside, California for a while and go to school there. Jim was twenty-one and still in the Air Force, Military Police, K-9 Unit at March Air Force Base. He and Teri were both in the Air Force when they first met and had not been married long when I arrived on scene with all my baggage — literally and emotionally. When I moved into their charming little one-bedroom bungalow, I slept on the couch in the living room. When they rented this home they had not figured on anyone moving in with them. They were both neat-freaks and I wasn't. It wasn't long before I felt overwhelmed with rules.

I was enrolled as a junior at St. Francis de Sales High School in Riverside, California, an all-girls school — another Catholic school taught by the Dominican Sisters. It was difficult for me to start again in yet another new school, having to make new friends. I kind of kept to myself and just let others befriend me. I must have looked kind of lost one day when a Sister came up to me and said that she could tell I was artistic by the shape of my eyebrows; and, did I want to take her art class? That one nun, reaching out to me in that simple manner, kindled a spark in me that would carry me through a lifetime of interest in creativity I never knew I had. I am sure it wasn't my eyebrows at all; I believe now, the

Holy Spirit used her to show me something different about myself. But at that time all I thought was, why not, what have I got to lose?

It took a while, but I eventually had a few friends that I could hang out with after school. We would go to a drive-in and sit and drink cherry Cokes®, smoke and gossip. That was fun. My art teacher was the only nun that cared about me. All the others would get on my case because my skirts were too short, my hair was bleached or I wore sleeveless blouses that weren't acceptable. More rules…

I don't recall how I managed to meet a boy that went to Notre Dame high school across town; but I did, and he asked me to the junior prom! He was tall, handsome and so sweet. The prom was a little bit of heaven and I felt every bit a princess. It was soon after that, he moved away with his family, I believe to Alaska, but I'm not sure; I just know it was really far away. We promised to wait for each other, but that didn't happen.

The highlight of my junior year was to model for a Seventeen magazine fashion show and to go to my junior prom. The rest of the time was difficult for me because I lived in the country and had lots of chores to do before I had permission to go out with my friends. I thought I was being used as a slave by my brother and sister-in-law. I was expected to iron my brother's stiffly starched fatigues. He was so particular about how they were ironed that they had to be perfect and without any wrinkles or creases that weren't supposed to be there. His shirts had to have two creases down the back measured exactly to his specifications and when he put on his pants, he stood on a chair, so as not to bend them; seriously. Teri had a specific way that the towels had to be folded, the floor had to be swept, mopped and waxed; etc, etc and on and on it seemed.

Jim trained K-9 dogs and it was my job to clean out each of the kennels, feed and water all the dogs before I went out for the night on a date. Sometimes I would still be out cleaning the kennels when my date came to pick me up; and then they would have to sit and wait for me to clean up and get ready to go out. That happened more times than I would like to remember. By then my brother was out of the Air Force and had become a Police Officer for Riverside P.D. So while I would be getting cleaned up, he would be interrogating my date.

Dates then weren't really what I think of as a date; instead, it usually ended up being a bunch of us piling in one car and going to the drive-in. Sometimes we would have alcohol and sometimes not. When we did, I drank like everybody else, even though I couldn't stand the taste of straight whiskey, or whatever it was. When I got home I would sneak in the house. Nobody was up waiting for me and I would just pull out the couch and crash. No questions asked. If I was out with friends and my brother happened to be working that shift, he would pull us over just to let my friends know he was watching. I wasn't even safe when he wasn't working because he would have his co-worker buddies do the same thing. Back then, it was embarrassing, but looking back, I see it was a godsend.

When the school year was out, I went back to stay with my mom in San Francisco; Jim, Teri and I needed a break from each other. Mom had moved again, this time to a nice two-bedroom apartment in a building with an elevator. It was on California Street, which was closer to her work. John, the Hungarian refugee, had moved in with her and rented the second bedroom. He gave me the creeps. He was around a lot when my mother was at work. He shared with me that when we lived in Seaside, he used to peek through the French doors of my mother's bedroom that led to my bedroom on the front porch, and watch me dress, and he told me how excited that use to make him. He also told me how he couldn't wait until I got older so that he could marry me. By this time, he was now in his forties and I was sixteen. I told him he was disgusting, but I never told my mother about the conversations I had with him.

Towards the end of that summer, I had become intimate with a young soldier that was shipping off to Korea soon. It was my first sexual experience, other than kissing and making out; and while I knew it was wrong and I felt guilty afterwards, I truly believed that we would marry when he returned home.

I don't know how John found out, but one night after my mother had gone to bed, John confronted me with the fact that he knew that I had had sex. He acted as if he were a jealous lover and flew into a rage telling me that if I didn't have sex with him, he would tell my mother what I had done and it would kill her. I was frightened and repulsed at the same time. I had already caused my mother so much grief that I couldn't live with her anymore. I felt I had no choice. He took advantage of me every chance he got. He would offer to take me places I needed to go so that it seemed to my mother to be helpful, and she would be grateful. I couldn't tell her; John had convinced me that my mother would never believe me. His abuse lasted until I went back to Jim and Teri's to begin my senior year. I didn't tell anybody; I was too ashamed to share this awful secret. I felt I brought it on myself; I had sinned and John was my punishment.

I soon got into the habit of ditching school with some of my friends every now and then. We would cruise around, trying not to get caught; go to the drive-in, smoke cigarettes and hangout until school was over, then meet up with everyone getting out of school and hangout some more. It was fun, because school was just something I had to get through and at the time seemed pretty meaningless.

I had acquired a boyfriend, of sorts, and we all called him Sugar. I liked him mostly because he had a car and was very sweet to me. On this one occasion, Sugar and about four other kids and I decided to skip school. We got hold of a couple of tall cans of beer and went out and spent the day in the country. Sugar brought me home that afternoon, and as we came in, the phone rang. When I answered, it was a woman on the other end that I didn't know, yelling at me that she knew that I had skipped school and that there was alcohol involved and the nuns were going to be told and I would be in a lot of trouble. I still don't know who it could have been, but guess it was a very angry mother of one of the kids that was with us that day.

At that very moment an overwhelming feeling of dread came over me and I was instantly filled with fear and anguish. I felt worthless and hopeless. I just couldn't get it right and life was without any purpose or meaning for me. I could not contain my secret any longer and felt I had no one to confide in. I dropped the phone and ran to the bathroom and locked the door. Sugar had no idea what had just transpired but knew I was in great distress. I remember looking through the medicine cabinet as I had done once before. There were no pills, but there was a razor. I had only time enough to slash one wrist before Sugar broke down the door. I think I remember just yelling, "I don't want to live," over and over again. What happened next was a cataclysm of pent up emotions. Somehow Sugar managed to reach someone that told him to get me to the hospital, and keep pressure on my wound to keep me from bleeding to death. I fought him as he struggled to get me in his car and then to keep control of it and me all the way to the hospital.

When I became aware of my surroundings, I was weepy but calm, laying on a gurney with a bright light overhead; my brother, in his police uniform, looking down at me. The doctors had stitched and wrapped up my wrist. Had no one been at home with me, I could have bled to death. I talked to him about how the nuns didn't like me, how I always seemed to be in trouble for some infraction of the rules, either by the way I looked or dressed.

The problem now was what to do with me. As law enforcement, Jim said he was duty bound to write a report and that I would be sent to a mental hospital for evaluation; or, he wouldn't have to write a report if I agreed to go stay with my mother for a couple of weeks, and if she agreed to the arrangement she would be responsible for me. I didn't want to go to a mental hospital — but I couldn't be with my mother because John still lived with her. I had to tell Jim why I couldn't stay with mom; I couldn't keep my secret any longer. He asked me if mom knew about what John did to me and I told him no, I had been warned not to.

I am told that when Jim let my mother know the whole story, she was devastated and was going to kick John out of the house immediately, have him arrested and he wouldn't be around anymore. It would then be safe to go home. I went to be with my mother and felt relief that John wouldn't be there ever again. I would find out later, however, that he was indeed still in my mother's life, but stayed away when I came to visit her. I never understood why she allowed him back into her life, or why she didn't press charges as she said she would. Maybe she didn't believe me. Maybe he lied to her. It hurt so very deeply that my mother seemed to side with him! We never spoke of it again. That two week stay with my mother is now a blur. I recall nothing of that time with her.

I returned to Jim and Teri's to finish my senior year of school. The nuns then had good cause to really dislike me because a detective was sent to their convent to investigate their treatment of the St. Francis de Sales students in general, and me, in particular. With my secret no longer burdening me, I slowly began to heal emotionally. Although I was attending a Catholic school, I still wasn't going to Mass on Sundays, nor did I have a personal relationship with Jesus. I was just going to try to be good. I limped through the remainder of the year and at graduation time, I had one short-hand assignment to turn in and I was through. I received my unsigned diploma on graduation day with my brother, sister in-law and my mother to cheer me on. Later that summer I would mail in my completed assignment of one page. My high school credits were then approved, and I was finally a valid graduate.

I was going to go stay with my mom; but first I wanted to stop off in Monterey and visit with my best friend from grammar school days. When I left there, the next stop was to go to Fresno and look up that super-tall, handsome jock that I had swooned over my freshman year but wasn't yet allowed to date. It just so happened that a girlfriend from my senior class also had family in Fresno, and she was also going there to visit; so I stayed with her. Once I got there, as soon as it was politely possible, I searched the phonebook for that guy's phone number. Bingo! My heart was racing as a man answered. It was him; and yes, he said he remembered me! He asked me if I was allowed to date yet. I told him I had just graduated the month before and would only be in Fresno for a couple of days before heading to San Francisco. He asked me out for that evening. I was in seventh heaven! It didn't matter where we went; the fact he asked me out set my heart to flutter. I dressed up as maturely as possible, wearing an evening dress, nylons and heels. My friend did my hair and make-up and I thought I looked amazing. I remember he was right-on-time, and the sun was just beginning to set. It was good to see him; he looked so handsome. We rode around for a while. No longer familiar with the area, I had no clue where we were or where we were going.

It was dusk when he pulled into some kind of orchard. I was really puzzled. Then I was alarmed when he parked and shut off the engine; we were out in the middle of nowhere. He moved towards me and suddenly his handsome face looked evil. I was petrified. He began to get aggressive. I fought him and began to cry. Then he shoved me to the floorboard and penned me there and began to laugh at me and said, "You know, it would be really easy to kill you right now." Then he uttered another wicked laugh.

Just as suddenly as it all began, he let go of me. As he slid back over to the driver's side, he told me I wasn't as grown up as he thought I would be. Without another word, he drove me back to where I was staying and dropped me off. As I stood there shaking and dumbfounded, I tried to process that it was just moments prior, I thought I was going to die at his hands; and off he went without seeming to have a care in the world. He was right — I wasn't grown up at all, and I wasn't sure if I ever wanted to be grown up. It was a terrifying night that I never talked about and put out of my mind for over fifty years, until now, as I put it on paper. I left for San Francisco a couple of days later, to live with my mom and feel safe.

What to do with me? I wasn't college material, didn't know what I wanted to do or be. My mom suggested I go to business school and be a secretary like she was. I tried and failed because it didn't interest me in the least. I began volunteering with the Red Cross as swimming instructor at the Presidio Army Post. My grandmother had moved across the bay to Fort Cronkite to look after her nephew's seven children who had recently lost their mother. Their dad was a career military man and was gone long stretches at a time. It was thought that I could be a lot of help to her looking after my little cousins. They were all under about ten or eleven years old, and as sweet and precious as could be. I began taking them with me to the indoor pool at the Presidio, where I was teaching young children to swim. They were able to sign up to learn to swim also.

My mother was eager for me to find a career of some kind that could make an income. I still had not found my niche, but I thought I would give hair a try, so I signed up at Marinello Schools of Beauty in downtown San Francisco to become a beautician. I stuck it out for as long as I could. Most customers were satisfied with the job I did; but the one or two a week that couldn't be pleased would make my blood boil. It was not my calling. My mother was frustrated with me because I never seemed to finish anything I started and I still had no solid goals that I was working toward.

To be honest, I had no idea what it was that I could do; what I could accomplish; what was out there for me to explore or even what my capabilities were. I was just taking it day by day. I had no thought that she wanted her own life and that I should be out on my own. But God had a plan for me; I just didn't know it yet.

PART 2

Kenneth Lewers Voorhees
3/31/40 – 6/1/68

Chapter One

OUR BEGINNING

The summer after graduating high-school, in July 1961, at the age of seventeen, I signed up to be a volunteer for the American Red Cross; that's when I first met "him." My job was to teach little kids to swim in the indoor swimming pool on the Presidio Army base in San Francisco, California. Ken was a lifeguard in the Army at that very same swimming pool. After a few days of teaching kids to put their face in the water and blow bubbles and to learn to float without being afraid, I happened to look up at the lifeguard stand and caught him staring at me. Then each time after that, I would just smile at him and he would smile back. It wasn't long after that little bit of innocent flirting, he drove beside me as we were walking to the bus stop to head back over the bay, and he offered me and my slew of little cousins, a ride home. That meant a trip across the Golden Gate Bridge to Fort Cronkite, a fair distance out of his way.

I was rather glib as I accepted, and all eight of us piled into his '55 Chevy, and in the back seat, the kids began devouring his bag of potato chips they found there; and off we went. I had no idea accepting that invitation for a ride home would begin a new and exciting chapter in my young life.

He had just finished a three-year stint overseas in Korea, and was going to be discharged from the Army soon. He then planned on moving back to Long Beach, in the southern part of California, where he was from originally. When we arrived home safely, I wouldn't allow him in the house until he met my grandmother, and she wasn't home. I said he could wait outside in his car until then if he wanted to; and he did. It was the next day before my grandmother came home and she wondered why in the world some guy was sitting in his car parked in our yard.

He met my grandma. She scolded me for making him stay outside. I told her it wouldn't look proper for him to be in the house with all the kids when I didn't even really know him. His staying out there overnight waiting for my grandma and respecting my wishes endeared him to me.

Our first date was a Giant's baseball game. I couldn't tell you now, who won or who they played. I wasn't into sports at the time, but that would soon change because Ken was a huge fan of Major League Baseball. He was a diehard LA Dodgers baseball fanatic and loved watching football as well!

We hit it off instantly, finding we had many things in common and not much that we disagreed about. We looked as if we could be brother and sister. He had the same color hair as my natural color, and he had blue eyes, too. He was about five feet eleven but preferred to say he was six feet tall. He weighed about 180 pounds and was well built. He told me about the girl he was engaged to when he joined the army and how she sent him a Dear John letter while he was overseas; his heart was crushed. He said he had promised to marry a Korean girl and that when he got back home, he would send for her. Her heart was crushed.

Ken became a great friend and confidante; so easy to talk to! I told him all about my crazy teen years and about what John, the Hungarian, had done to me. None of what I told him swayed him at all; he was crazy about me. Nothing I had ever done in my past mattered or changed his opinion of me. He had much compassion and understanding for what I went through with John. Ken was my first experience of being cherished and loved unconditionally. It was new and it felt wonderful!

He surprised me three months later, in October on my eighteenth birthday, with an engagement ring. As we rode the rickety old elevator up to my mother's third floor flat, he proposed to me, and I said yes. It was a couple of weeks later by the time we came up with a wedding date, February 3rd, 1962. I was so excited that when I got home, I woke my mom to tell her the news about the date for the wedding. Her first reaction was, "why so soon?" I guess she was relieved that I wasn't pregnant. The next day she and I began making plans for the big day. Ken wasn't Catholic, so in order to be married in a Catholic church, we had to go to pre-nuptial counseling for six weeks, and he had to agree that our children would be baptized and raised in the Catholic faith.

It was decided that to save a huge expense, I would wear my sister's beautiful wedding gown and my sister-in-law Teri's veil. The bridesmaids and groomsmen would rent their formal attire, which was another savings. My step-dad, who had financially helped with my sister's college and her wedding, did not offer to help me in anyway, nor would my mother ask him. I chose my brother Jim for the honor of walking me down the aisle. He and my sister-in-law helped me live through some of my roughest teen years when they themselves were barely in their twenties and newlyweds on top of that. It was no easy task for them for sure.

When February 3rd arrived Ken and I were married in beautiful St. Dominic's Cathedral in San Francisco. My mother did an amazing job planning and providing a fairytale wedding for me on such short notice and on her single-parent income.

Our guest list was kept modest to include only immediate family and close friends in order to be affordable for my mother to have a catered sit-down brunch at the reception. The setting was the famous Cliff House in San Francisco that heralded spectacular panoramic views of the beautiful Pacific Ocean. It was a dream of a reception, fit for a prince and princess. It was a perfect day in every way.

We transitioned from single into married life quite comfortably, living in an apartment in San Francisco for a short while until Ken was discharged from the Army. Being

newlyweds was one of our happiest of times, only to be sur-
passed by the birth of each child to come from our love. Ken
was discharged from the military within a couple of months
of our wedding and was hired immediately at a meat packing
plant in Oakland. It was time to pack up our meager belongings and move nearer to his job. We settled into a modest
two-bedroom apartment with a pool in Hayward. There was
one small problem; children were not allowed. I had just discovered that I was expecting our first baby. We would be able
to enjoy it for awhile before we would have to move again.

Life was good. I was so happy and content being a wife
and excited about becoming a mommy! My sister and her
husband lived within a couple of miles from us, which meant
lots of sister time while our husbands were at work. It was
beyond exciting when we discovered we were both pregnant
and our babies would be so close in age. She and I spent a lot
of time together and our bond grew ever stronger.

All seemed to be perfect, so I was startled when I began
to have one horrid reoccurring dream. It was so bizarre and
unsettling to me that I never felt I could share it with anyone,
especially with Ken. It just didn't make sense to me and
scared me even to acknowledge it to myself. I kept trying
to put it out of my mind, but the dream kept coming back.
I dreamt that there came a knock on our door and when I
opened it, there stood two policemen. They were sorry to
have to tell me my husband had been shot and killed.

My dream took me step by step through the shock of
hearing the news, arranging his funeral, and even the grief

of being a widow. But it was all nonsensical and crazy, I told myself; and I refused to put any stock in it at all. We were young, happy and crazy in love; it was absurd to even think of such a thing. I had no idea it was a dress rehearsal for things to come.

Scotty was born in October of 1962, and soon after we had to move from our "no kids allowed" apartment complex. We bought an adequate three-bedroom home on the GI bill, with no money down. It had lots of room including a bedroom just for our new baby boy. The spare bedroom would soon welcome our second baby that was on the way. Yes, that's correct, as we celebrated our first anniversary I was already six weeks into my second pregnancy. Scotty and Roxie were ten and a half months apart.

Ken was an only child, and his mother thought that since we had a little boy and a little girl, we had the perfect and complete family. So she made an offer for us to sell our home and come to Southern California to live. We could move into the house that they had purchased and renovated in Lakewood; all we had to do was just take over the payments. They would then move into Ken's grandmother's cottage across town so they could be her caretaker. We made the decision to accept her generous offer. We sold our home for what we had invested in it, and off we went 400 miles south — not a job nor a prospect of one; two babies, and not a care in the world that together we couldn't conquer.

When we first arrived in Lakewood, Ken took a job as a cabdriver. That was short lived after he was held up twice at gunpoint in just a matter of a few short months. We didn't wait for a third time to decide that it was much too dangerous an occupation. He confessed that he would miss the time between runs when he could park his cab under a street light and read his Bible. He knew he had too much responsibility as a husband and father to take the risk of staying in that line of work.

By 1966 we had four little ones; Scotty was four, Roxie was three, Rusty was one and Ronnie was a newborn. Ken tried his hand at several different kinds of jobs but he decided a good stable career choice with a steady income would be a firefighter. He applied, and while we were awaiting the call for an opening with the fire department, he was offered a manager's position with Kentucky Fried Chicken. Working at Kentucky Fried Chicken as store manager meant many hours away from home; sometimes 12 to 14 hour work days. But he was never too tired when he got home to swoop up each child and love on them, pile them in the car and take them to the park, play catch with Scotty, push Roxie on the swings, or wrestle with babies Rusty and Ronnie on the grass. That was my time to catch my breath.

I was at the point where I was a bit overwhelmed with my lot in life; I didn't know I was pregnant again until I suffered a miscarriage at six weeks. My hormones were all out of balance. I went to our church to speak with the parish priest about my situation and how overwhelmed I felt. I was expecting sympathy and compassion, anything but the advice I got! He told me to go home, be thankful my family was healthy and quit whining and complaining. He added, do something productive and clean out your kitchen cupboards to work off some of your anxiety. I was horrified that he would tell me such a thing and not offer me one word of encouragement or comfort. I guess he thought I was selfish, spoiled and had too much time on my hands, and maybe he was right. However, that did nothing to correct what I saw as never-ending mounds of diapers, laundry, and ironing, with no end or relief in sight.

One night when Ken came home from work, after having worked about a 12 hour shift, I told him that I had decided I needed to leave him and take the children with me to my mother's boarding house in San Francisco. I will never forget the crushed look on his face. It was as if I had stabbed him in the heart. He was devastated. We talked and cried throughout the night and come morning light, I had a much better perspective of things. We both agreed that some time with my family would be good for me and for the children.

While I was gone, he planned to surprise me by putting on a fresh coat of paint on all the interior walls in our house, nice soft neutral colors. His mom and adoptive dad would paint the exterior of the house, and would let me choose any color I wanted, when I got home. Yes, I guess I was spoiled.

During my stay in San Francisco, Ken and I exchanged sweet love letters and progress reports; from me, it was about the children and from him, it was about the house. After nearly a month apart, the children and I were anxious to come home. And what a sweet homecoming it was! The house was in perfect order and Ken had worked so hard to make it look so warm and inviting! We renewed our commitment to each other and fell more in love than ever. The year was 1967.

We celebrated our sixth anniversary February 3rd, 1968. When Mother's Day rolled around that year, we signed the Mother's Day card for Ken's mom, *with love, Skip (it was Ken's nickname his family called him), Pam, Scotty, Roxie, Rusty, Ronnie and?* We had taken the coward's way out rather than tell her face to face and chance being the object of her wrath. It took her a moment to realize that it was our way of announcing that we were expecting another baby. Oh, gracious, was she ever mad. She said we played a dirty trick on her and she was not delighted with the news at all. We understood her concern because she knew we were struggling financially and "just couldn't afford" another child. My mom used to say, "If people waited until they could afford to have children, nobody would ever have children." I guess it was a good thing Nana never knew about the miscarriage I had just a few months earlier; she could barely speak to me or look at me as it was. But, that would soon change.

Chapter Two

THE CALL

It was Memorial Day, 1968 and my brother Jim and his family made the seven-hour drive down from Boulder Creek, to spend the holiday with us. It was always a happy occasion to have family come visit. It was evident by the squeals of laughter coming from nieces, nephews and our kids spending time together, playing and running all over the house, that they were having a grand time. Because Ken had to work, my brother decided to go by KFC to visit him and catch some of the LA Dodgers baseball game on the radio. Ken was an avid Don Drysdale fan. Even I grew to know that both Drysdale and Sandy Koufax were two of the greatest pitchers of their time! I knew that because as far as I was concerned, Ken was pretty much an expert on baseball stats, and he said so!

It was such a fun visit that when they packed up and got ready to leave Saturday morning, I was sad to see them go, but they had a long drive home and Jim had a doctor's appointment the following Monday morning. I remember it being one of those fun times you just don't want to end, filled with happy-go-lucky memories.

As night manager for Kentucky Fried Chicken, Ken was often scheduled to work holidays and at least one weekend night every week. June 1st was a Saturday and he was scheduled to work from early afternoon through the evening dinner rush, and then was responsible for closing out the register after all the other employees had gone home. He would then stop and make a deposit of the daily receipts at the after-hours vault at the bank on his way home. It had become routine for him, and he reassured me often that he would always be vigilant of his surroundings and wouldn't put himself in harm's way while making his late night deposit. He was a cautious man and his reassuring words somewhat set my mind at ease. He didn't want me worrying needlessly because it wouldn't be healthy for me or for the baby.

Jim and family left for home that morning, and Ken was off to work in the afternoon. I managed to get through the afternoon lunch time and dinner hour pretty smoothly, but by bath-time and bed-time for four little ones, I was exhausted. I was only three months pregnant, but my energy was completely depleted by nightfall. So, after I had the kids all tucked in for the night, I went upstairs, knowing I would probably fall asleep on the couch watching TV while waiting until Ken got home from work.

It was late, around 11:30 p.m., or so, when the phone rang and woke me. I had fallen asleep on the couch as usual. Ken had not come home yet. As I answered the phone, a man on the other end identified himself as the night janitor for KFC. His words seemed to run together as I tried to shake loose the fog of sleep in my head; something about having found the store's back door open; and going inside, he said he found my husband in a kneeling position just beneath the store's electrical box. It didn't dawn on me what it was he was trying to tell me. The room began to spin as he ended by saying that he wasn't sure, but he thought my husband was still breathing when the ambulance took him away to the hospital.

I dropped the phone and flew down the stairs and out the door into the dark of night, running up and down the street like a crazy wild woman, not knowing what to do. I wanted to scream, but I didn't want to wake anybody and scare them. I ran to my neighbor's porch across the street and couldn't bring myself to knock on their door; it was late, I didn't want to wake them and worry them. I couldn't call my mother-in-law and tell her on the phone what I had been told. I wasn't at all able to think or grasp what it all meant. I had to get to the hospital to make sure that Ken was going to be okay, but I couldn't leave my sleeping babies home alone. I finally ran back into the house and called my neighbor, shivering, crying and apologizing for waking them — I didn't know what else to do. Two of my friends came at once and stayed with my children while their husbands drove me to the hospital.

We rushed into the emergency room entrance and at the same time a doctor emerged from behind one of the curtained areas. He walked right up to me and asked if I was Mrs. Voorhees; I acknowledge that I was, and then with all the sympathy and compassion he could muster, he said that he was sorry to have to tell me, but it appeared my husband died instantly as a result of electrocution from the electrical panel at work; would I be able to make a positive identification of his body, he asked. I went numb and was no longer able to stand or speak. My neighbor, Ron, who with Howard brought me to the hospital, volunteered to make the identification for me. I was given a sedative by injection and taken home. My friends made all the necessary phone calls for me to Ken's mom and step-dad, my mother, brothers and sister. My children slept peacefully and innocently through the night not knowing they would never see their daddy again. In a blink of an eye, our lives were forever changed.

It was a couple of days after Ken's death that the Medical Examiner completed an autopsy. I was notified by Sheriff's detectives that Ken had not died of electrocution but had been shot; the single bullet from a .357 magnum had pierced his left arm and his heart, killing him instantly. They were now investigating a homicide and robbery. My brother Jim, who had been in law enforcement for several years, drove back down from Boulder Creek to help me in any way he could. He and my brother Joe took it upon themselves to keep up with the investigation into the search for Ken's killers. Relatives and friends were looking after my children, while my mother and mother-in-law went with me to make funeral arrangements and see about financial assistance.

Ken's mom, Nana to our children, lost her one and only beloved child; I knew the pain that I felt was unbearable; I couldn't begin to imagine hers. My heart broke for her.

I didn't look pregnant yet, but Nana wanted to make sure that everyone attending Ken's funeral knew that I was pregnant, so she bought me a new maternity dress fitting for a funeral. She was now thankful for all of her grandchildren, even the one yet to be born. All past hard feelings on her part instantly melted away, and we began to bond closer than ever before. We needed each other; my children needed her, and she needed them.

My most difficult task was how to tell my children. Ronnie and Rusty would turn two and three that month and were so little they didn't understand where daddy was, but they sensed something was not right. I struggled over how to tell my four- and five-year old that their daddy was killed by a very bad person. I did it as delicately and briefly as possible. Scotty had been anxious when I put him to bed the night of June 1st to tell his daddy in the morning about a great baseball play he had made that day; but he would never get that chance. He was the oldest, and I feel it left an indelible scar which he was never able to overcome. Roxie, being the only little girl in the family, was her daddy's princess. She longed for the special attention he had paid her. She had always felt safe and secure in his arms. I made the decision that the children didn't need to go to their daddy's funeral. I wanted them to remember him as he was the last time they saw him.

I don't remember much of the day of the funeral. In fact, there are very large chunks out of my life around that time that I have no recollection of at all. It wasn't until just a couple of years ago that I connected on Facebook with a young woman who told me she wanted my email address so that she could write me a letter. She said she used to babysit my children. I didn't remember her. When she emailed me, she revealed that I had taken her into my home when she was a teenager. She actually lived with me, and I don't remember. But there were so many personal things that she knew about each of the children and me, there would have been no other way for her to know. She wanted to apologize for taking advantage of me, because she had disrespected me by bringing her boyfriend into my home when she knew he used drugs. I had no idea of any of this. She lives in Texas now and has a beautiful family and grandkids. We still keep in touch. My hope is that someday my memory of those times will come back. But maybe God has a different plan. My only explanation during that time that is blocked from my memory is that God was working in me and through me to help someone else, when I wasn't even aware of His presence.

The children were so resilient, trusting and loving in what I characterize as living life in a new kind of normal. I realized that they looked at me and mimicked whatever mood I displayed. If I talked with excitement, it made them excited. So, that is what we did. We had the excitement of going to church on Sundays, then stopping by a flower stand for carnations and going to the cemetery to bring daddy flowers and remember him; then off we would go to Nana and Papa's house for "Papa breakfast!" This was a very happy memory, and still to this day, "Papa's breakfast" is a favorite to fix on Christmas morning, or for any special occasion.

I wanted life to be an adventure for my kids and for them to know that we would always be a family, and we would get through whatever came our way. Six months later, I was preparing them for their new little brother or sister. I had chosen two names, one for a boy and one for a girl. Whatever gender this baby was, the name Kenneth was going to somehow be incorporated into his or her birth name. Relatives and neighbors were still checking in on me and helping me out with household chores and giving me a hand with the kids.

Friday, December 13, 1968, Kenneth Daniel Voorhees was about to make his debut into the world in grandiose fashion. With the kids at home in my mother's care, my neighbors, Ron and Howard (yes, the same ones that made the trip to a different hospital with me in June) volunteered to rush me to the hospital as I was in active labor. They both sat up front and I had the whole back seat to myself. I didn't think I would make the eight or ten mile trip to the hospital. I begged them to pull over so I could just have the baby right there, somewhere on the side of the road. They kept telling me, "hang on, hang on, just a little bit longer!" They spotted a police car, flagged him down and asked for a police escort to the hospital, to which the officer replied, "It's against our agency's policy." Howard then spoke up and asked the officer if he knew anything about how to deliver a baby!

Well, some rules are made to be bent when necessary. I had a full-blown escort, red lights and siren the rest of the way. As I lay in the back seat looking out the car window, all I could see were bright shining Christmas lights and decorations, reminding me that I was about to receive the greatest of all gifts, Ken's last child.

We made it to the hospital parking lot where there were several people awaiting our arrival. All of them rushed toward the car, each jockeying for position so they could see in the car windows. I was trying to keep my modesty, but that was a lost cause. The doctor jumped in the back seat, mumbled a few cuss words and in less than a minute, helped welcome Danny into the world. He quickly handed him off to a waiting nurse who hurriedly whisked him away before I could even see him, as the crowd that had gathered around the car cheered him on. It was a bit of a different delivery, to say the least, with Danny deciding the back seat of our neighbor's car was a way more cool place to be born on a Friday the 13th then some plain ole ordinary hospital.

I was helped onto a gurney and wheeled into the hospital where they took me to a room on the maternity floor for observation. A short time later Ron and Howard came into my room to see how I was doing, both of them looking like proud daddies. The doctor and nurses wanted to know which one was the daddy. And just for a brief moment, the three of us were profoundly saddened because in celebrating the miracle of Danny's birth, we were reminded that this little one would never know his daddy.

I was given something to help me rest peacefully through the night. I was not aware until the next morning that my newborn was fighting for his life due to aspiration pneumonia. A priest had been called in and administered to Danny boy what Catholics called the Sacrament of The Last Rites or the Last Sacraments for the sick and dying. There were blessings prayed on his life through the next few hours by priest and staff. By morning he had made it through the night and began to make remarkable progress. He had excellent care, and I was able to bring my healthy Danny boy home a few days later.

Now there were five little ones for me to nurture and care for; a reason for me to keep living, even though some days were really tough, and nights were agonizingly lonely. Many times I didn't feel up to the task and didn't think I was capable of raising my children alone. There were days I didn't want to keep going, I just wanted to give up; then, all I had to do is look into their precious, trusting and innocent little faces and I knew somehow it would be okay.

A Poem by Pam

Gone forever, but yet so near, I blow a kiss and I can feel the sweet return of heavenly love. With my worldly eyes wide open, I cannot see what is in store; but with them closed a heaven I see, with my loved one at the door. His work is done and mine begun, to follow with strength, the will of God. And then, one day my turn will come, when sadness and sorrow will be no more. By: Pam Edison Voorhees 6/19/68

PART 3

James "Scott" Voorhees
10/19/62 – 8/2/87

Chapter One

OUR FIRST BORN

K en and I had been married less than a year when the first of our five children was born. Scotty, as we called him until he was about twelve years old, was an adorable baby with a shock of blond wavy hair, bright smiling blue eyes and a Gerber baby face that would make any new mama puff up with pride. He sure looked to be perfect in every way as far as his daddy and I was concerned. I wrote the following little poem sometime during the nine months we were anxiously awaiting his birthday:

> *Oh little one who is yet unseen,*
> *except in all my fondest dreams;*
> *I see your little hands and feet,*
> *so soft and lily white,*
> *your precious face so heaven-like,*
> *and your cry that's oh so sweet.*
> *You are all that mommy wished for,*

and so very soon the time will come
when you'll be here for all to see;
why you were in my fondest dreams.
By "A Mommy to be" October 1962

I was one week shy of turning nineteen, and on top of the world when Scotty was born, but I had not the first clue about babies or what to do with them. I found it astonishing that the hospital was going to trust me enough to let me take him home with me. But after five days, they did just that; they turned us out on our own to go home and live happily ever after.

This fair-haired child was a delight and definitely the cutest baby I had ever laid eyes on; and he was mine! He did everything earlier than all the parenting books said he would. And, when he discovered he liked the taste of magazine pages, I thought that was a sure sign he was going to be an avid reader; he was even walking by the time he was nine months old and into everything. It was a full-time job just keeping up with him. He was so ahead of his time, I knew he was destined for great things. He was a star. He was the apple of our eye. He easily adapted to big brother status in 1963 when he was ten and a half months old and we introduced him to his brand new baby sister, Roxanne Marie, Roxie for short. He loved her immediately, just as we did, and was never jealous of the attention we gave her. I had my hands full with both of them, for sure; but they were such a delight!

I would dress them up, put them in the buggy and off I would go to meet my sister and her two little ones, Shane and Toby. We would stroll around town with our babies, proud mommies that we were! Those are cherished memories. By 1966 our family expanded to include two more babies, Rusty and Ronnie, both June babies born a year apart.

Scotty quickly became the center of attention by becoming a Los Angeles Dodgers fan, watching intently with his daddy on game days. And, before he started school, he was able to memorize and recite the names of most all of the players on the team and their individual stats. He loved the game and he wanted to learn how to play, so his daddy obliged him; and every chance he had, they either went to the park or out in the yard to play catch and practice his swing.

He began kindergarten early; he wouldn't turn five years old until six weeks after school started. The nuns at the school where I was trying to enroll him wanted me to keep him out for a year. I thought he was much too smart to waste time waiting and so we made the decision to put him in public school so he could get started. He had no problem keeping up academically. Socially, he may have been a bit more immature than the rest of the class, but that didn't seem to bother him either, as he made friends easily.

Life was good in the Voorhees household. Here we had in our first-born, an intelligent, athletic, witty, funny and fun-loving little boy. He loved school, baseball and playing with the neighbor kids. He and Roxie were always together, keeping busy and never bored. I am not quite sure who the culprit was, or if both were, that thought it would be fun to light matches under the bed and set the mattress to smoldering. All I could think of was what *could* have happened, but didn't. That was just one of many occurrences of heart-stopping magnitude that kept me awake at night, and always on my toes, trying to ride herd on such a large family; like the time two-year-old Rusty climbed out of the second story window and stood on the roof; or the time three-year-old Rusty stuck his hand in a portable ice-crusher and mangled his tiny little fingers. Then there was the brush fire Rusty and his cousin Mike started in the field next to our house; and the time Scott came back from riding our Shetland bare-back and showed me his dangling arm, bent in and S shape where there was supposed to be a bone. I suppose I could fill this book with heart-stopping events such as that; but, bottom line — their guardian angels were kept busy watching over them and they did a mighty fine job of it. The icing on the cake, they were all adorable and each one melted my heart. It was difficult for me to reprimand with any consistency because I still felt the pain they endured losing their daddy, and because they were each so precious, even when they were naughty. When in anger, I began to yell at a child, calling him/her by name, I had to go through all their names before I got the right one; they would laugh at me, and I had to laugh at myself. Yes, I suppose they probably got away with a lot more than they should have when they were younger, and I was probably a little more laid-back than I should have been.

Scott and his sister and brothers were all taught to be polite, mind their manners and be respectful, and they generally displayed these habits in public very well; I guess that's where it counts the most. Scott was my very favorite child; that is, until Roxie was born, then she became my very favorite too, um, then Rusty came along, well of course he was definitely my favorite too, until Ronnie came along, and oh wow, he was my number one all-time favorite too, and then Danny boy, shot to favorite status instantly; oh wow, then five years later Justin became my very favorite also. Those of you who have more than one child understand how each of your children can be your very favorite.

After his daddy was killed, Scotty was never quite the same care-free little boy he once was. I think, looking back, he tried to step into Ken's shoes and be the little man of the house. I tried my best to keep my household as close to the same as it was when their daddy was living, but I failed miserably. I won't go into all the mistakes I made; let's just say I made many poor choices trying to recreate a family unit that included a daddy in my children's lives. What I discovered was, no man could take their daddy's place, nor love my children as their daddy did. My choices were all for the wrong reasons, not out of unconditional love, but out of desperation to be a normal family again. My children in turn, suffered because of all the poor choices and bad decisions I made. That's not what I wanted for them. I wanted them to be happy. I wanted a normal happy family once again.

By the time Scott was in the third grade, we moved to Redding, a beautiful little town in northern California where the Sacramento valley meets with the majestic coastal mountain range to the west, Mt. Shasta to the north and Mt. Lassen to the east; and the added bonus of the beautiful Sacramento River running right thought the middle of it. It was to be a new start for us as a new family unit. In 1973 we welcomed a sixth baby into the family. Justin was my fifth baby boy. The kids were all pretty excited about it. Roxie had been praying for a little sister; but that was not to be. Her disappointment lasted only until she got to hold her new little brother. Justin would be my last child. Six was the perfect number of children for me. I joked that I gave Justin his name because I had decided I wouldn't have another baby after I turned thirty, and he came "just in" time. About three months after Justin was born, our family dynamics changed once again. It was a very trying time in our lives, but the kids were resilient, as always seemed the case. We managed to survive and move forward. At the time, only God knew how it would all work for the good in our lives, in spite of me, and in spite of our situation. The details are not important at this juncture and perhaps it is a story left for my children to write one day. I will acknowledge that looking back I can see where the hand of God was in our lives and all up in our business through it all.

Scott was already a super athlete in youth baseball. He was a natural, and he made it look effortless on his part. He played shortstop and catcher and was outstanding in both positions and his batting average was right up there with the best of them. Back then, you had to try out to get picked by the coaches to be on a team. When his try-outs came, it was with a cast on his left arm. It was almost healed and we had permission from his doctor to try-out. He had broken his arm about six weeks earlier when his horse spooked and bucked him off. He had to have surgery to set the break. He still had to wear the cast for another couple of weeks, but it didn't stop him from making the team.

After baseball season he decided he wanted to learn to play guitar. I think I bought his first acoustic guitar from a pawn shop. He learned how to play chords in school and did so well that I paid someone to come to our house and teach him to read music. It was no time at all and he was playing songs I recognized and playing them very well! Then the young man I hired to teach him advised me that Scott was very gifted, but he wasn't reading notes; he was playing by ear. The lessons ended there, but the playing would continue throughout the rest of his life. It was another gift that he made look effortless; it was also his love and his passion. He formed a small band and they practiced every minute they could. They played in the parking lot of grocery stores, under the stands at the State Fair, for parties and anywhere anyone would have them.

Scott and I were very close. I was probably overly protective of him, trying to make up for the loss of his father and the unfair treatment I felt he received from step-fathers. I made excuses for him because of what I had put him through in relationships I had with men who were jealous of him; they thought the attention I gave to Scott should have been to them. Choosing step-fathers to fit what I perceived would fit my children's need of a loving two-parent home, was all for the wrong reasons; but it didn't stop me from trying.

As close as mother and son could be, I still didn't know that by the time Scott was thirteen, he already had a drinking problem. I was blind to the ramification when I discovered he had been drinking before baseball practice. I had come early one evening to watch him play baseball and he wasn't on the field yet when they were warming up. A few minutes later, I saw him as he emerged from between two apartment buildings across the street from the park. He had alcohol on his breath. I made the decision right then, to go ahead and let him play and make a fool of himself to teach him a lesson. I would let the coaches handle the situation as I was sure he would be discovered. He played ball that night; never missed a beat and probably played one of his best games. It was definitely not the lesson I had hoped he would learn. My experience with drinking at an early age jaded my thinking, because I did not grow up to have a drinking problem; I figured it would be no different for him. In high school though, he began cutting classes, hanging out with "the wrong crowd," drinking, smoking pot and generally wasting his teen years and his talents. Except for smoking pot, he did very little different than I had done at his age. I never understood why, though. He was gifted in so many things and had so much potential that he was way ahead of me, and had so much more going for him than I did. He had natural ability in music and sports, and loved both with a passion.

When he was old enough to drive, he got his first job working at McDonald's, and it was there he met and fell in love with his future wife. I saw hope then, because she was very good for him. He eventually was able to help pay for his first car, his gas and his car insurance. Looking back, I must have been in denial because to me, he was utterly charming, funny, witty, athletic, musical and a wonderful loving son. I have no words to adequately explain it; inside he was still my precious son and when he acted out, I had to share in the blame for it myself.

I had married yet again in 1975, but it was the period between 1978 and 79 that were the toughest for me and I believe for Scott, too. My husband and I argued a lot over how to discipline "my" kids; he had a short fuse and I had a sharp tongue, an ugly combination. We didn't see eye to eye on the subject of my children at all. To the outside world, we appeared to be a fairly happy, normal family. However, the cauldron was simmering deep inside me as I found myself on the defensive all the time about how to discipline or treat my children, especially Scott. The father figure I had chosen to complete our family was a nurturing, warm, fuzzy kind of father to his two children, and that was exactly what I wanted for my children; but it was much too much a monumental task for him. He felt duty bound to make sure they grew up to be respectful. He was a decent and good man to my kids and when it came to sports he was a very enthusiastic supporter of Dan, but was at his wits' end with Scott.

At one point, when Scott was nearly seventeen and a junior in high school, the three of us got into a fierce argument, over what I haven't even the slightest recollection, but my husband gave me an ultimatum that Scott would have to go, or he would leave me. In the heat of the moment, as a mother wanting to shield her child from any further hurt, it was not a difficult choice to make; I would choose my child over any man any day. Once again, I had failed my children.

Scott came to me a few days later and asked me to sign permission for him to join the Navy. He had just begun his senior school year, and because I insisted that all my children attend summer school for extra credits, Scott already had enough credits to graduate. All he needed was to take a history test and he would receive his diploma and could join the Navy. And he did just that. My heart was shattered to think that my son would want to go off and join the military. I was sure it was to keep peace in the family, and maybe it was just to escape his life at home. He convinced me that this was what he really wanted to do; he would learn a trade, see the world and it would change his life.

He was inducted into the Navy on his seventeenth birthday, and then he was gone. I cried for weeks when he left, but only on the inside, trying to keep up a good front by laughing and smiling on the outside.

I wrote in my little pink journal, the following when he left October 22, 1979, as follows:

Scott has joined the Navy. I am both sad and proud. He is so young to have taken such a decision. I will miss him more than I can say, it hurts to let go. And, then I think ahead in the not too distant future, of having to let go of each and every one of my children. Please God, give me the strength to do it gracefully. I love them and thank you each day for allowing me to be their mother.

On a sad note, the summer after Scott joined the Navy the Philadelphia Phillies came to town looking for Scott. They had scouted him the year before and were looking forward to seeing him again. It broke my heart when I shared the news with Scott. It made him feel he missed out on an opportunity of a lifetime for his dream of someday becoming a pro.

In all fairness to the man I was married to during this time, he was exceptional in many ways. Where I went wrong in the choosing is that, he wanted a wife for himself; his children had a mother already; my children had no father and that's what I wanted for them, a father. He thought he had found what he was looking for and I thought I had found what I was looking for. We were just looking for different things. I wanted a father for my children that would love them unconditionally as I did. As much as I loved them, I never thought just my love alone could ever make up for them not having a daddy to love them, too. My five boys needed a strong male role-model and my princess needed a daddy to spoil her.

Subconsciously I felt they were cheated out of a loving two-parent family. I kept trying to make it up to them, trying to recreate what we all once had. God allowed me to blunder through life, learning everything the hard way. Even at that, some things still took years before I realized I needed to quit steering my life and my children's lives in every crazy imaginable way I could think of, and let God be the pilot. I was one that didn't want to bother God with small stuff if I thought I could figure it out myself. The truth is, I didn't feel worthy to even ask Him to sort out the mess I was making in my life.

Now Scott, the one child that got car sick at the mere mention of mountains and curvy roads, instead of joining the Army, Air Force or Marines, opted for the Navy and signed up for duty on a nuclear submarine. He loved it! He came home on leave, and at eighteen years old, married his high-school sweetheart. Yes, the sweet young girl he met at McDonald's! Shortly before he celebrated his twenty-first birthday, his life consisted of a beautiful wife, a precious baby boy and a full-blown love affair with Jack Daniels. He signed himself in the Navy's drug rehabilitation program on base, where he and his little family were stationed in Connecticut.

My husband and I made the cross-country trip to visit him and his family in Connecticut for his twenty-first birthday. He was given a weekend pass to spend at home with his family. During our visit he shared horror stories about the many times he came close to dying due to his drinking, but each time he had managed to cheat death one more time. He couldn't shake the lure of alcohol and the power it had over him. He tried quitting several times on his own, only to get angry that others could have a drink socially without having to keep drinking. He wanted to be like that, but it had a different effect on him. He always had to have more. After his four years in the Navy were up he re-enlisted for another four years. Then, for reasons unknown to me, that plan changed and instead he and his wife and baby came back to Redding, California and civilian life.

His wife never complained to me about Scott's drinking, but it was obvious that it had to be a difficult life for her, at best. He was not reliable if he was drinking, and although he had no trouble finding employment, he was never able to hold a job for any length of time. Then he would feel guilty and try to get sober on his own will-power. That never worked. I noticed he began having mood swings; one day he would happy-go-lucky, charming and witty; the next day he might be sullen and dark. He loved his wife and little boy as much as he was capable of loving anything in the world he lived in. He wanted more than anything to be a good daddy, but he didn't know how.

His wife gave birth to their second child on New Year's Eve, 1985. He was ecstatic about this new and perfect little baby boy and so proud! But, it became an excuse for him to celebrate. It was not long afterward that he basically abandoned his family, and nobody knew where he was. After quite some time, he contacted his wife, and would continue to do so sporadically, but she could tell she was losing him. A few months later he called me and said he couldn't go on living the way he was living and needed help to get sober. The man that wanted him out of our house just a few short years before was the same man that now wanted to do what he could to get him help. Scott said he would be coming up from Los Angeles and would meet us about half-way. We agreed that we would work out a plan together for his goal of sobriety, once and for all.

His life was a complicated mess, and he would need to be sober in order to make coherent judgments and decisions. He now had a girlfriend in Los Angeles, and she was pregnant with his baby. He also had a wife and two little boys in Redding. He knew he had hurt those he loved, and was overcome with remorse and guilt. He wanted to do right by his boys and by the baby that was on the way, and he knew he couldn't do anything to repair the damage he had done until he fixed what was wrong with him. I had no answers for him other than to give him the help he asked for to get sober. I was riddled with my own guilt about all the things I could have and should have done differently.

Somehow I knew that a lot of his pain was my fault. I spent a life in denial of what was probably painfully obvious to everyone else. What kind of mother was I? I would have to face this at some point and ask God about it, but not right now. Right now he needed to get sober so he could work through all of it for his future and the future of his children.

There was a beautiful mountain lodge half-way between Redding and the Pacific Coast that we checked out for Scott. It was a rehabilitation facility for alcoholics and drug addicts. The setting was gorgeous and serene and the people were warm and friendly; it seemed the perfect place to get sober and get his thoughts and his life together. Scott agreed to go, and we wasted no time getting him checked in, guitar and all. I was cautiously optimistic; but there was still a matter of this thick cloud of guilt that seemed to follow me and weigh heavier and heavier on my mind. I would have to deal with it, later.

Scott seemed enthusiastic and filled with a hope I had not seen in a very long time. It was, however, to be short-lived. He wasn't there but a month when we got a call from his girlfriend's mother that his girlfriend was in danger of losing their baby and was in the hospital. She needed to contact Scott to let him know. Instead, we said we would tell him, and we did. It would then be his decision to contact her, and he did.

His girlfriend's mother wired Scott money for bus fare back to southern California. Scott walked away from his chance at sobriety that day, hitched a ride to the bus station in Eureka, and headed south. It's what he felt he needed to do. I was angry with that mother for years, decades even, for sending him that money. All hope went out the window because of that one act. It was easier for me to be angry with her than to admit that Scott made the choice and be angry with him. He had a wife and two precious little boys that loved and needed him. Yes, his wife still loved him and wanted him back home to be a family again.

Now, his girlfriend loved him and needed him, too. Her pregnancy was a difficult one, and Scott felt he needed to be there for her. That was a decision he had to make for himself. Several months went by and Scott became daddy to a beautiful, healthy baby girl. All seemed as if Scott had worked it out in his own mind how the future was going to be. It was a situation I didn't want for him, but I would have to accept if I wanted him to continue to be a part of my life. My heart ached for his wife and my sweet precious grandsons; had I known how bad the situation would become, my heart would have ached for my little granddaughter and her mother, too.

Chapter Two

THE DREADED CALL

It was my day-off when the phone rang on the evening of July 27th, 1987. It was from my daughter Roxie. I was single again, just recently divorced and living in Anderson, California with my youngest son who would be attending junior high school in September. I worked for Anderson Police Department as an e911 emergency dispatcher. Roxie lived about 500 miles away in Chatsworth, California, so it wasn't unusual to get a call from her. We were in the habit of chatting back and forth on a regular basis. This call, however, was immediately different; her voice was strained and desperate. Through uncontrollable sobs, she began to tell me about her brother, my oldest child Scott. "Mom, (*choking on sobs*) Scott tried to kill himself tonight." More sobs and sounds of anguish made her words stilted and foreign to me. My mind could not grasp what she was trying to tell me. It was unbelievable, and I was unable to process it at first. My mind and my world began spinning out of control. I had to regain composure as I had been trained to do in my job as an emergency dispatcher. I had to detach so that I could understand and retain all the information I was receiving. It was all at once as if I were talking to an hysterical stranger about a horrible tragedy. I was used to dealing with it day after day, and learned to remain calm and quick thinking; that was my job.

But this was different; this was my daughter telling me about my son! As she continued, she managed with much difficulty to tell me what she knew . . . something about Scott had been drinking all day and had gone to his apartment, tied a rope or a tie around his neck and then looped it around something in the attic and hung himself.

My heart stopped and time stood still, but my mind continued to race. I was not able to absorb what I was hearing. It was as if I were somebody else eavesdropping in on a party-line, listening to a stranger's tragic story. She was still choking out words as I snapped back into what would become my new reality; I heard her saying he was still alive when his girlfriend found him and cut him down, and the paramedics rushed him to the hospital. Roxie's words began to run together and my head began to swirl. She was saying something about him being put in an induced coma because his alcohol content was so high he would be going through severe DTs. They had no idea if he suffered brain damage. They had no idea if he would live or if he did, for how long.

I quit trying to make sense of anything. In a daze, I hung up the receiver, my brain not wanting to process what my daughter had just told me.

Chapter Three

SAYING GOODBYE

I borrowed money from my brother Joe to fly down and be with Scott. My daughter Roxie, my brother, my sister Penny, my new granddaughter and her mother were all at the hospital. There were others, but I no longer recall who they were. The rules were very strict in the ICU and they weren't about to bend them; I waited my turn to see my son.

I hardly recognized him with his head restrained, his neck in a brace, and his arms and legs tied down. He was on a ventilator and a chest tube was visibly protruding from his side. Other lines and tubes seemed to surround and invade him from all directions.

My first five minutes that I was allowed with him, I wasn't able to let myself think that he was dying. He was in a coma. All I could tell him was how much I loved him, and how I wished I had been a better mother. I prayed to myself, "Lord I ask that you heal him from this horrible addiction to drugs and alcohol which has enslaved him; and Lord, if he will never be strong enough to overcome, I pray you take him home." I couldn't bear to see him this way and I couldn't bear the thought of him struggling throughout the rest of his life battling this demon. I surprised myself that I was able to pray those words and mean them. It was not until many years later, when giving my testimony, that I was able to share that I had said that prayer. I had feared people would be shocked that a mother could earnestly pray those words over their child.

I asked my daughter if Scott had been seen by a priest and she said no. I asked her to request that one come see him, pray for him and give him the last rites. I don't know why I couldn't bring myself to ask for a priest for him, myself; but I couldn't. I didn't leave the hospital. I stayed in the ICU waiting room in between my short visits with him. I didn't want to miss an opportunity to see him. My daughter-in-law had given me a letter to read to him when the time was right, and so I did. It was a letter of love and forgiveness that I read to him when nobody else was around. I don't know if he heard me; but I understand that people in a coma can hear. I believe he did.

The priest did arrive and prayed for Scott and gave him the last rites. By morning, Scott had regained consciousness. His restraints were taken off and his neck-brace removed. He was alert and wide awake but unable to speak due to the ventilator and the damage done to his vocal cords. The nurses let us come in together as a group to see him for just a few minutes. He tried to sign a few words, which he had learned from his sister-in-law, but nobody could interpret, so he gestured for a pen and paper. The first thing he wanted to know is if he hurt anybody. Then he joked, he couldn't wait to go home and have a beer. Nobody thought that was funny, and we told him so. They kept taking him out of the room for tests and to measure his brain waves. They were astounded that he was so aware of his surroundings and able to recognize all of us.

That night we could tell that he was beginning to slip back. I believe it was my sister Penny, Roxie and I at his bedside when he asked if he was going to die. We acknowledged that, yes, it would be soon. We asked him if he believed that Jesus Christ was his Savior and died for his sins, and he nodded yes; then he was asked if he wanted Jesus to forgive him, and he nodded yes. We cried and we prayed as he slipped deeper and deeper into a coma. By morning he was being kept alive by machines.

I said my farewell to my precious blond-haired, blue-eyed first-born son. I could not bear to watch him take his last breath. I flew back home and began to make funeral arrangements as I waited for the doctor to call me with the news that he had passed away. I was expecting and prepared for that call; but I still fell to pieces, crumpled into a useless heap, my heart shattered, when I heard him say, "Your son passed away peacefully this morning." That was the second of August, 1987.

Scott's three beautiful, precious children would now grow up without knowing their daddy — as did he, and as did I. In my heart of hearts, I don't believe he wanted to die. I believe he just wanted the pain to go away. The devil thought he had him; but he was a child of God, and God snatched him from Satan's grip and claimed him for His own. Though my faith was scarcely the size of a mustard seed, I was able to recognize, even then, God's hand in Scott's living and in his dying.

Chapter Four

SCOTT'S SONGS

S cott loved to play his guitar and sing, and I loved to sit
and listen. In the beginning the songs he created were
fun, lighthearted and catchy. He would sing while strum-
ming, and then stop in the middle and jump to another tune
that popped into his head. Everybody took great delight
in his antics. He would just have fun with it and not take
himself too seriously.

When I was his only audience, he sang my favorite,
Led Zeppelin's "*Stairway to Heaven*," and an assortment of
songs by John Denver, Elton John, and a little Pink Floyd.

He loved Pink Floyd, and who didn't? I thought some
of it was kind of on the dark side; or maybe I was just being
square. The truth is, I was probably in denial.

I wasn't aware of the dark and sinister songs he wrote
until they were shown to me after his death. The two that
follow were written at different times; one he dated 1982,
when he was about 20 years old. The other was dated 1986,

when he was nearly 24 years old. They are the only ones I know about that so devastatingly depict his struggle with weakness, alcohol, drugs and self-loathing.

Written by Scott–1982
No Title

I lie awake at night my eyes are burning red,
I think that I'd be better off living with the dead
Sometimes I hear a whisper,
Often times it's clear,
The voice I hear is frightening, but it's a voice I cannot fear,
The voice is always telling me the things that I do wrong.
I just can't seem to block it out, it's like a sickening song,
It's tearing up my insides, aching in my brain,
The truth the voice will tell me is driving me insane.
I like to drink that whiskey,
It makes it seem OK,
But the voice just lies inside me 'till the whiskey goes away.
I think my life is over 'cause I think I finally see,
The voice inside I hate so much……………………..
Is really only me.

Written by Scott–1986
Cocaine

1) *I picked you up*
   I held you high
   You couldn't leave me
   You wouldn't try.

2) *We've been together*
   For so long
   How can you think
   That it's so wrong

3) *You can't survive*
   When I'm not there
   You'd kill yourself
   Cause you don't care

CHORUS: Don't forget about me
Cause I'll drive you insane
Don't call me nothing fancy
Just call me cocaine.

4) *The first time you met me*
   You were sitting in a bar
   You needed someone special
   You didn't look too far

5) *I set my hooks into you*
   And spun your life around
   And when you were done with me
   I slammed you to the ground (back to the chorus)

6) *Please Mr. Cocaine*
   Can't you hear me cry?
   I just want to live again
   I'm much too young to die.

My Poem for Scott

A mother's love begins at birth, transcends death and reaches into eternity. Her love knows hope, joy, pain and sorrow. There will be no shrine for glory – only <u>one</u> brighter star in the heavens for this mother's love to see.

By: Pam Edison Voorhees 8/6/87

PART 4

Patrick Ronald "Ronnie" Voorhees
6/23/66 – 4/2/89

Chapter One

THE QUIET ONE

I believe I carried Ronnie for ten months before he was
born. My doctor gave me a May due date, but he wasn't
born until June 23, 1966. Going into the tenth month, I tried
all the tricks, going on bumpy car rides over railroad tracks,
drinking castor-oil, ugh, and even walking around the block
a few times; but he wasn't going to move until he was good
and ready. I knew before he was born that he would be
Patrick Ronald Voorhees and we would call him Ronnie. I
loved that name; it sounded so Irish to me – well, except for
the Voorhees part, which added a bit of Dutch and German
flavor to the mix.

They didn't do any tests back then to tell me if I were
having a boy or girl. I didn't believe any of those old wives'
tales about how to determine the gender; I just knew. Roxie
was still hoping she would have a little sister, but when
Ronnie finally made his grand appearance to the outside
world, she adored him.

He was a gorgeous baby boy, of course. He had lots of reddish blond hair that framed his little round face, and chubby cheeks that everyone wanted to pinch. He had tiny little ears that stuck out a little more than his sibling's did when they were born. At first, I tried taping his little ears back; I guess my thinking was they needed to be trained so they would stay that way. His skin was too sensitive to the tape, however; so I decided I would just leave his little ears alone to be whatever they would be. They actually just made him that much more adorable.

I have to say, he was probably the best little baby out of all of them. He was so good natured; he never demanded much attention; maybe because his sister mothered him all the time. Roxie was almost four years old when Ronnie was born, and he was better than any doll she had to play with. Having four little ones under five-years-old was quite a task for a young mother, so Roxie's help was quite welcomed.

It helped that we lived in a wonderful tree-lined neighborhood with a lot of young families, something right out of a Norman Rockwell setting, I would say. Our house was on the corner and the usual gathering place for all us young moms to sit on the front lawn, visit each other, and chase after our kids. Life was a bit hectic at times; but it was good to be able to share daily stresses and stories with other mommies. I remember one incident with Ronnie when a little girl of about three came running up to me breathlessly, and with a thick southern accent blurted, "Tha lil fa bowa stole ma tracycle!" Yup, that was my sweet little Ronnie. He was so used to sharing with his brothers and sister; he thought it would be okay to share with his little friend.

Ronnie was just three weeks shy of two years old when Ken was killed. He never got to know his daddy. I am comforted in the reality that Ken knew, loved and cherished each and every one of his children, even the one that was beginning to form within me. The initial impact of losing their father was greater for Scotty and Roxie because they were older, at four and five years old. All of the children ultimately suffered the ramifications of losing their father. They were raised off and on by men I chose to try and fill their daddy's shoes — men who didn't love them, cherish them or know them like their daddy did.

Ronnie loved school and was fastidious in his work and his penmanship. The only naughty thing I can remember him ever doing was while he was in Cub Scouts. They had a "Guess How Many Beans Are in the Jar" contest and Ronnie proudly guessed the exact number. When he went to accept the prize, they asked him how he figured it out to the very last bean. That's when Ronnie broke down and started crying as he confessed he saw the answer written on a piece of paper that he wasn't supposed to see.

Ronnie was a lovable, sensitive, compassionate and caring young boy. He always had a sparkle in his eyes and a smile on his lips, with just a hint of shyness that endeared him to all he met. His irresistible dimples were an added bonus. He was eventually able to overcome his shyness, and as he grew, his personality just soared. He danced to the beat of his own drum; he did not follow — he led. He was agile and loved playing baseball and football; but being an athlete wasn't his passion.

He prided himself in accomplishing things that were kind of out of the ordinary. He figured out how to solve the Rubik's Cube puzzle and was able to master it in seconds, leaving his brothers and friends scratching their heads and wondering "how'd he do that?" He would happily proceed to show them how it was done. He mastered the hacky-sack that was popular in the seventies. In his young teens he decided to learn how to ride a unicycle. He started off with the regular size and then graduated up to the very tallest one he could find. When he mastered that, he taught himself to juggle while riding his unicycle.

He knew how to have fun and was pretty much the life of the party. He and his buddies he hung out with managed to stay out of some of the mischief that most young teen-agers get into.

Russ was fourteen, just a year and twelve days older than Ronnie, when Scott enlisted in the Navy. Russ wanted to learn to play guitar like his older brother, and Ronnie wanted to learn how to play drums. That Christmas they got their wish; Russ got a guitar and Ronnie a set of drums, all bought from a pawn shop downtown. Along with that came music lessons. Russ learned to read music, and spent hours and hours practicing. He had the passion and perseverance and learned to become a terrific guitar player through his efforts. Ronnie did the same with the drums — practice, practice,

practice — until he became an accomplished drummer. He even joined the high school band so he could get in more playing time.

He began to be a fashion guru of sorts and bucked the trends of the day. He mixed Levi's and a t-shirt with a gray top-hat and tails for school dances, and sometimes while just hanging out with his friends. Whatever he wore was uniquely his style. Ronnie grew to be rather tall at six feet three. He had a slender build, but broad at the shoulders. I was told that he looked a lot like a young Nick Nolte. He was very popular. He never picked up the habit of smoking or drinking. He didn't need to; he was comfortable being himself, and he knew how to have fun and make people laugh.

Russ, Ron, and their step-brother decided to form a band; their own rock band. They were crazy about the music of the band, "Rush." They lived, ate and slept Rush music. When it came time to think of a name for their own band, they knew they couldn't copy the name of their all-time-favorite band, so they decided to call themselves "Sequel," which meant to them a sequel to Rush.

During high school, both Russ and Ronnie worked at McDonald's. Yes, the very same McDonald's where big brother Scott first worked and also their sister Roxie; a family tradition it seems. Russ wanted to move out as soon as he graduated; but a year later he was still at home and going to junior college. When Ronnie graduated the next year, he, Russ, and their step-brother paid a visit to the Army Recruiter at my suggestion. They said they would do it to humor me, but no way would they be signing up. That afternoon they came busting through the door all excited about the high scores they each received on their ASVAB test! They said they signed up for four years and were guaranteed to be together all through boot camp.

My husband and I surprised them by showing up in Kentucky for their boot-camp graduation. What a proud moment that was! It was also the first time I had ever witnessed fearsome aggression in Ronnie. It happened after the ceremony. We were all in a reception area when Russ and my step-son had to forcibly stop Ronnie from pouncing on a fellow soldier. Ronnie explained to me that "Nobody disrespects my mother and gets away with it!" I don't know what that young man said to upset Ronnie. I am glad Ronnie stuck up for me; but I am doubly glad that Russ was there to help defuse the situation.

After the basic training, and their MO training, they found that they would all three be stationed in Germany, together! That had not been promised. Soon after they got settled in, Ronnie asked to have his drum set shipped to him. And before long, Sequel was playing at all the local pubs near their base. They even had t-shirts made up that said "World Tour."

Back at home, Justin, my youngest, had taken up Ronnie's flair for style. He wore jeans, t-shirt, top-hat and tails to his eighth-grade dance. He was stylin' and he was a hit. When all three Army boys came home for Scott's funeral, Ronnie was the one who paid special attention to Justin, mentoring him and taking him places, being a loving big brother. That really stuck with Justin — I wouldn't realize how much until later.

Back in Germany after the funeral, Ronnie wrote to me that he wanted me to come to Germany. He would buy the plane ticket and give me the grand tour of castles and the Alps and all of Germany. I thanked him and said I just couldn't do that. I don't remember what excuse I gave him. Bottom line: the real reason was fear, paralyzing fear, pure and simple. I couldn't tell anybody the real reason, because intellectually I knew it was silly. But true fear does funny things to a person's psyche, and it wreaked havoc with mine. I was afraid of flying by myself, and afraid of going to a foreign country not knowing the language. I will always regret that my fear kept me from an amazing time with my son.

Ronnie was good natured about it. He never let me know he was disappointed, although I am sure he must have been. He had a lovely girlfriend back home, and he made her the same offer; she accepted. He wined her and dined her and treated her like a princess, to the extent, I am told, he laid rose petals on her bed. Ronnie never grew out of his "preciousness."

Russ and Ronnie were as different as night and day; yet the four years they spent together in the Army created an unbreakable bond between them. It was a closeness that began at home and grew into genuine friendship, love and respect for one another. Even when Russ married the love of his life soon after boot-camp, it was Russ, Deanna and Ronnie that went everywhere together.

They were boys when they joined the Army in 1984, and they were men when they were honorably discharged in December of 1987. While they were away those four years, a lot happened. My mother died in 1986. Three months later, Ken's mother died. A few short months after that, I divorced again. Then, in August, 1987, Scott died, leaving two darling little boys and a grieving widow, as well as a precious baby girl and grieving girlfriend. Roxie had married, and soon her five year old son was big brother to a little sister. Russ was married, and they had a sweet little baby girl. Yes indeed, a lot of things happened in a short amount of time.

One of the first things Ronnie wanted when he got back in the states was a new truck, and he wanted me to be a co-signer. He had already picked out a brand new Ford Ranger. I didn't believe it was wise to co-sign for something I couldn't afford if I had to take on the payments. I told him I wouldn't be able to do that for him. He was just out of the Army and looking for work. It was too risky for me to take on, as I still had Justin at home to provide for. Ronnie was okay with that. The mother of one of his buddies offered to co-sign for him, and offered for him to come live with them, rent free. That was a bargain I guess he couldn't pass up; after all, I lived in the mountains twenty miles from Redding. It wouldn't have been convenient for him to live that far out of town.

Rather than appreciate what she did for him, I harbored resentment for years toward this woman because I felt she had out-bid me, depriving me of precious time with my son.

Ronnie was ecstatic with his brand new beautiful truck and was just beaming when he showed it to me. It was gorgeous and I could see why he felt so proud.

Chapter Two

THE UNTHINKABLE

∽❧◈☙∾

I loved my cute and cozy little two-story wood-frame home in the foothills east of Redding. It was right at the snow line at 3,000 feet. In the winter it was like a picture postcard. Justin loved it, too, because he had a four-wheeler that he could go off for hours in the woods and explore. I had been dating Ben, a man that worked for the city of Anderson, where I worked at the police department. We had fun together. He was divorced and had a teenage daughter about Justin's age who was still at home. Ben loved to go hunting, camping and four-wheeling. Perfect, I thought; just what Justin needed in his life, a father figure that loved the same things he did.

It was a Sunday morning, April 2, 1989, when I got off work after covering the graveyard shift at the Police Department. Ben came by and asked me if I wanted to go to a swap meet before I headed up the hill twenty miles in the opposite direction to go home. It sounded like fun. I knew

Justin, being a pretty typical fifteen-year-old boy, would no doubt still be sleeping until I got home. It felt like a great day to do something spontaneous, and a swap meet seemed just right.

We made our way through the crowd of people, meandering from table to table, picking up everything at each booth, then setting it down and going on to the next display and doing the same thing. When we got our fill of that, I suggested we go visit my daughter-in-law Mary, Scott's widow. She had just had surgery a couple of days before, and was still in the hospital. It seemed a good time to stop by and say hello and see how she was doing.

When we arrived in her room it became instantly still, as though time had stopped and everyone was frozen in their place. The room seemed to be crowded with Mary sitting up in her hospital bed, her mother standing beside her, then standing in sort of a semi-circle coming around from the foot of her bed, were my daughter Roxie, my son Russ, his wife Deanna, along with a few other faces I no longer recall. In the room as well, I would learn quickly, was the hospital chaplain. Their faces turned ashen as they faced me and all of a sudden I felt dread overcome me and my knees wanted to give way. A voice broke the silence; *"Ronnie has been in an accident, it's not good. He didn't make it."*

I stared blindly, incredulous, as the words I heard began to sink in. How could this be? I had already reached the depths of a dark, wretched and bottomless pit when I lost my oldest son just twenty months prior. I had not even fully come to grips with the reality of losing him and now I am being told my precious Ronnie was dead too? Ronnie had only been back in the states for four short months! I was sure I could not survive this blow; but I was wrong — I began my descent into a living hell as I spiraled into a vast abyss.

What happened? Was anyone else hurt or killed? Where, when? And the story of how I lost my son began to unfold. As gently as possible, the chaplain put his arms around me and told me that Ronnie was driving northbound on I-5 towards Redding, in the early morning hours when his truck veered off the Interstate into the median, flipping over several times and ejecting Ronnie out of the window, killing him instantly. I would discover later, through police reports, they surmised he probably fell asleep at the wheel and the vehicle gained momentum in access of 80 miles per hour when it left the road. Ronnie wasn't wearing his seatbelt.

My next thought was to go home and get Justin. I dreaded telling him. I wouldn't get the chance to tell him — the tragic news wouldn't come from me; it came in the worst possible way. The office of the Coroner, looking to contact the next of kin, checked with my employer and was told I was off duty and might be home. The Coroner then called my house, and when Justin answered, the man on the other end asked Justin if I was home. When told no, he then asked if Justin knew Patrick Ronald Voorhees. Justin answered in the affirmative that Ronnie was his brother. The man then identified himself as David N., from the Coroner's office, and proceeded to tell Justin that his brother was killed in an accident earlier that morning. What a horrific way for a young teen to hear the news of the death of a brother he cherished! The impact of that message would leave him with an indelible scar.

Before shock could consume him, he instinctively called his brother Russ and blurted out what he had just been told. That set into motion Russ making more phone calls and making arrangements for his father-in-law to go pick-up Justin as quickly as possible to be with family. Everyone went from the hospital to Russ's house to gather round and try to make sense of this horrible tragedy. When Justin arrived, he and Russ went to a service station near Russ's house, where Ronnie's truck had been towed. They felt compelled to see for themselves that this was real and not a garish nightmare. I couldn't allow myself go; my emotions were a mixed bag of shock, grief and anger! Yes, all of a sudden, I was angry that he got that truck because that woman made it possible for him to have it. Had she minded her own business, would Ronnie still be alive? These were ugly, bitter thoughts running though my head. I had to blame someone. I couldn't blame Ronnie, and I was afraid to be angry with God. The devil battled for my soul that day and every scintilla of my sanity was at stake.

Justin found Ronnie's leather jacket in the truck. Although it was torn and bloodstained, Justin wore it every day for the next two years, even throughout the summers, no matter how hot it got outside. It was a piece of Ronnie that he desperately clung to and cherished.

Dan had enlisted in the Army in January of that year, and was away in Kentucky at Fort Knox going through his

Advanced Individual Training (AIT). The Red Cross contacted him and he was given leave to come home. It was a whirlwind of activity, making arrangements and notifying everyone. I don't know what I would have done without my kids. Though they were grieving the loss of a second brother, they huddled around me, consoling me, as if to shield me from any further tragedy or heartache. My own pain was so unbelievably deep that I wasn't even able to be of comfort to them.

Unfortunately, I had gained experience arranging funerals. My first stop was to go to the credit union and take out another personal loan for $3,000.00, the same as I had done for Scott's funeral less than two years prior. That was the limit I set, that I knew I would be able to repay. I basically told the funeral director I wanted the same arrangements for Ronnie that he had done for Scott. Ronnie's would be a modest funeral with a simple service at the funeral home. His burial would be next to his brother at Whiskeytown Cemetery, a twenty-mile procession that would take us to the outskirts of Redding. It was a cemetery for poor people, mostly. I chose it because the setting was in the pines in the hills close to Brandy Creek at Whiskeytown Lake, where all of my kids and their friends had spent many memorable times.

Both at Scott's funeral procession and now Ronnie's, I insisted on driving myself, following behind the hearse. I didn't want to be driven; I needed to do this for myself, I was their mother. I had to be strong and stay focused. I tried as best I could to hold it altogether emotionally; but as their mother, the pain at times cut too deeply to visit that place in my heart that was forever shattered. I knew I had to figure a way to get through this and be able to function. I could only take it a piece at a time, a moment at a time.

Where was God in all my grief? I didn't dare to ask Him. I thought that the tragedies in my life were brought on by the rebellion of my youth and my sinful nature. This was my lot in life. This is what I deserved. I waited for more punishment from an angry God. My heart was heavy with guilt and shame, thinking I could have been a better wife, a better mother, a better person.

It is said that one shouldn't make any major decisions after experiencing a devastating loss. I guess nobody had the heart to tell me that. I made life changing decisions trying to create some semblance of normalcy. I was going full speed ahead, to anywhere that would take the pain away.

I returned to work, but with the realization that my life would never be the same. People would never look at me the same, and I would never look at myself the same. This was how my life was to be; anything but normal.

It seemed only a minute, and Justin was old enough to be on his own. There I was, a mother who no longer had any children at home nor any identity of her own. I continued to make relationship decisions that would prove fruitless and without rhyme or reason. It seemed I left a path of destruction at each turn in the guise of trying to be what I thought would look normal. My grief, despair and self-pity were drowning me beneath still waters.

Chapter Three

A TRIBUTE TO RONNIE

❦

From brothers, Dan and Justin
Written with love, respect and admiration

"Even though I have people to comfort me, without you here I feel like I'm standing in the middle of a ghost town. I know I can speak for everyone here when I say 'You were easy to love.' I have also realized that there was no way I could have ever told you I loved you enough. You meant so much to me as a brother. You were unique in every way. I truly feel sorry for the people that will never get a chance to meet you.

As strange as it may sound, I thank God for this pain, because one can only feel this pain when hearts are open. The time I spent with Ronnie is worth all the pain I can stand. It hurts, but our paths will cross again; only next time it will be for eternity.

I've heard life is like a jigsaw puzzle. If that is true, then why won't this one piece, known as tragedy, fit? For a piece with such a unique shape, it seems like it would be easy to find its place. Maybe it's because every time I come across this piece, I grip it so tightly, I change its shape. I have finally come to realize, this piece I hold goes to a puzzle of its own; to one only the holder can identify and relate to. I feel like saying, 'OK, now that I know this, Ronnie can come back,' but this is a life-long test. Ronnie passed that test when our brother Scott died because he recovered and lived the rest of his life as Ron Voorhees, the loving and completely caring person that he was.

I am proud of you and I'll always love you, Ronnie.

Written and read by: Dan Voorhees (age 20) on April 6, 1989

I have tackled my problems through thickness and thin,
I can barely see the light through the midst of sin,
The Lord has promised to show me the way,
Now I have a debt; I must kneel and pray.
My brother is gone but his soul remains,
He left us his trends of leather and gold chains.
Though his body lies deep in the ground
I'll always have memories of when he was around.
Ron was a drummer; he never missed a hit,
I hate to say this, but he made Neil Peart look like (.......).
When God came knocking on Ron's door,
He opened it up and saw what was in store.
He said he was pleased and give Justin my keys,
Now I shall be happy forever more.

Written by: Justin Voorhees (age 15) on April 13, 1989

My Poem for Scott Revised to Include Ronnie

A mother's love begins at birth, transcends death and reaches into eternity. Her love knows hope, joy, pain and sorrow. There will be no shrine for glory – only two brighter stars in the heavens for this mother's love to see.

*By: Pam Edison Voorhees * revised 4/6/89*

PART 5

Letting Go

Chapter One

MY LETTER OF GOODBYES

❦

Written September 1992

A counselor once told me that one of the best ways to get through grief is to write a letter of goodbye to all the things you have lost that were important. I am still grieving the loss of Ken after twenty-four years; the loss of my first born son five years ago; and the loss of yet another precious son three years ago; and so now, I will begin my long journey of goodbyes.

Goodbye dad; you left before I got to know you, before I could understand what real dads meant to a little girl. All I know is what I saw of other dads and what I conjured up in my mind. I guess I miss not knowing what I missed.

Goodbye step-dad; I thought you were my real dad until you left; real dads didn't do that. You abandoned me, yet told everyone how special I was. You did nothing for me in all the years that followed except express shallow sentiment every year or two. I was bitter, but as I stood near your death bed, I forgave you; you did the best you could and so, as I did then, again I say goodbye to you.

Goodbye to school friends that I went to grammar school with. I didn't want to leave. I want you to know I wanted to stay but the choice was not mine. Goodbye to lasting childhood friendships that might have been.

Goodbye Grandpa; you were so very special in my life. I can still see your kind, handsome and gentle face and beautiful gray hair. I miss your hugs. I miss sitting in your lap combing your hair. I miss you. I wish I could have told you how I loved you, before you died, but a twelve year old doesn't think of death and I never expected you to die. Goodbye.

Goodbye Ken; to our dreams we shared, the love we shared and the trust we built together. It's hard to say goodbye to a dream. We had only six years together; we were just getting started. I was only just beginning to mature. We had our whole lives ahead of us. We had beautiful healthy children that we adored; a beautiful home, wonderful friends, and each other. Now I have to say goodbye to the one man who loved me just as I was, with all my faults. I have never found another to match you; no one could measure up. It's so hard to let go of something that over the past twenty-three years I have envisioned as perfect. I know and you know it was not perfect. It was good and wonderful, but not perfect. Because I have not let go, perhaps through the years in my mind it has become perfect. I compare it to all that I have had and I can't do that anymore. Nobody can measure up to a fantasy. You have become my fantasy and I must say goodbye. I love you, Ken; I will always love you in my heart, but I must finally say goodbye and let go. I must find strength to move forward.

Goodbye Jared (not his real name); My dream world was built and destroyed in just a few short years. Some memories are keepers; the rest must be laid to rest, once and for all.

Goodbye Todd (not his real name); and to all the sadness, hurt, misunderstandings, friendship, trust and love. I am sorry my journey to heal didn't start sooner. Goodbye, I wish you well.

Goodbye Scott; I can only let go of the physical you, not the treasure of loving memories. I will say goodbye to the sadness, anguish and anxiety your drinking and drugs brought. If only you could have seen yourself as a wonderfully talented person, the way others saw you. What a joy and delight you brought to your children. Goodbye to the strum of your guitar and the songs you would sit and sing to me. In the still of the night, there are times I can still hear you singing "Stairway to Heaven." Oh God, you know how much I miss him. It is so hard to say goodbye.

Goodbye Ronnie; my strong and gentle giant. You knew how to live life large! You were always happy, challenging life with enthusiasm and always compassionate toward others. Your goodness was a gift to others. I miss your beautiful smile, your crazy and cool outfits, your charm and your wit. You were so much fun to be around whether you were drumming in a band, riding your unicycle, juggling or showing little kids how to master the things you loved to do. You lit up my heart with happiness. Losing one son did not prepare me for losing another. Goodbye my precious young man; I still miss you so.

Goodbye Ben (not his real name); I had no intentions of destroying your life. Goodbye to a relationship that was not right from the beginning. I had no idea that this would happen; but it did. Goodbye to all the pain, resentment and rejection that we each felt these past four years. Goodbye to you and a dream that I had.

Ken Voorhees – 1959

Pre-wedding picture with my sister Penny
and bridesmaids Teri and Diane

The new Mr. and Mrs. Kenneth L. Voorhees – 2/3/62

Scotty – one year, and Roxie – six weeks
1963

Pam and Ken – 1967

Scotty
Park League Baseball – 1968

Scotty and his baseball trophies – 1968

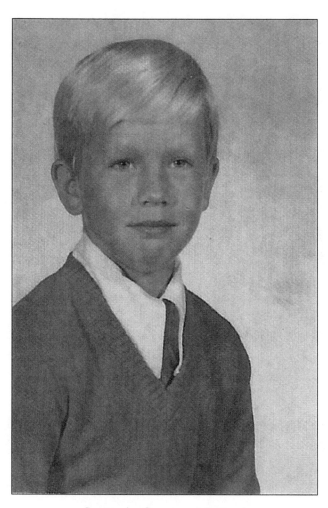

Scotty in Grammar School

Ronnie in pre-school

Scott – undated

Ronnie's graduation with big brother Scott

Ronnie's Army picture

Ronnie loved his drums

Brothers Russ and Ron, dress rehearsal for Russ's wedding

Justin, Ronnie, Roxie, Russ and Dan – 1987

This picture taken while Russ and Ron
were home on leave for Scott's funeral

PART 6

God's Grace Goes Before Me

JEREMIAH 29:11-13

This is the Word of God for the People of God

[11] "For I know the plans I have for you," declares the Lord, "plans to prosper you and not to harm you, plans to give you hope and a future. [12] Then you will call upon me and come and pray to me, and I will listen to you. [13] You will seek me and find me when you seek me with all your heart."

Jesus is Lord of All

Taken from the song, "Jesus is Lord of All" Lyrics by William J. Gaither and Gloria Gaither, the words that follow tell the story of where I am today.

All my tomorrows, all my past,
Jesus is Lord of all.
I've quit my struggles, contentment at last!
Jesus us Lord of all.

Chapter One

A SUBTLE WORK IN ME

W hat is it like to live a life filled with false pride, defined as that pride which is derived from the approval of others, which then may manifest itself as pretending to be somebody you are not; and self-pity, defined as self-indulgent dwelling on one's own sorrows or misfortune? Well, to paraphrase scripture in Psalm 10:4 it basically says, in your pride you don't seek him because in all your thoughts there's just no room for God. Now then, you have just finished reading how that way of thinking affected my life and many of my decisions. All of my schooling and my up-bringing was geared toward living a Christian life. Lord knows I had plenty of exposure to it; but, with the exception of my First Holy Communion, all the rest seemed to impact me either hardly at all or in a negative way. It was all about being a Christian which in my mind is different than being Christian.

The concept of "Born again," was foreign to me and conjured up the "Holy Roller" image. I wanted no part of that! I wanted to be somewhere in between pious and hell-bent. I didn't want to give up what I considered to be the fun things in life, and become some holier-than-thou naysayer. Besides, if the life I was living was sinful, I didn't think I could ever be anything but a sinner. And, with that train of thought, the next thought would nearly always be, why am I even here? How could God ever forgive me enough so that He could give me some kind of purpose? I was too far gone to be helped. Maybe if I could just be good enough or maybe if I could just do more good works to make up for every time I sinned, then maybe God could overlook the bad things I had done.

My sister Penny and I were and still are, very close. I looked up to her, but never thought I could be like her. She was my big sister, my protector and my shoulder to cry on. I could tell her anything and everything. Sometimes I told her things in a way just to shock her, to see if she would change her opinion of me. She never faltered nor condemned me; her love for me never wavered.

Later in our lives, we would make plans to meet, each driving a couple of hours to meet in a central location, somewhere half-way, and spend the day together . Our times together were happy and care-free and usually involved going to garage sales or thrift store shopping, or both. As the day wound down, we would pick a nice place to have a meal and a glass of wine and just talk about our lives. It seemed as though every time we did that, the conversation turned spiritual. She was a saint to me, and when she told me things,

I believed it; or sometimes, I just really wanted to believe, even when it seemed impossible.

She would remind me I was a child of God; that I was in His family; that my name was already written in the book of life, and that He would never let me go. I would sit across from her, listening; all of a sudden tears would well up and spill over without my understanding why I was weeping. My sis would just say, it is the Holy Spirit that dwells in you that is letting you feel His presence. It brings tears to my eyes as I recount those words, just as it did when she spoke them. It was so humbling! I wanted so very much to believe it but I just couldn't understand how that could all be possible. Although my sister knew me better than anyone else, there were still some things only God and I knew. I was just not worthy to be forgiven. And that's where I stayed stuck for decades; not feeling worthy of forgiveness, and falling short of being as good as I thought I needed to be.

Over the years, when in casual conversation with friends or relatives the subject of religion would come up, there would always be the question about one another's salvation status; to which, a lot of people said they knew they were saved. While I wondered how they knew, I could only say, "I hope so, but I will probably spend half of eternity in Purgatory first, before I will be fit for Heaven."

In 1996, seven years after Ronnie's death, I finally came to the end of my rope, and there was little left to hang onto. I had come to a point in my life that I found no hope for anything better. I was constantly making the same mistakes over and over, each time hoping for a better outcome. There was just an instant, while driving the curvy two-lane highway between Eureka on the coast and Redding, when I thought to myself, what would happen if I just aimed my car at one of those trees that lined the road? Wouldn't everyone be better off? It would look like an accident. With a thought like this even crossing my mind, I knew instantly I had to pull off the road. The words of the therapist that I overheard as a young child came to mind, and I was filled with fear that I may be losing control. These were not my thoughts; this was not what I wanted. I eased off the road and found a quiet place to park near a creek. There is something about the water in a stream, in rivers, lakes and oceans that soothe my soul. Although I didn't know it then, it is obvious to me now that God was with me.

Psalm 23: 1-3 comes to mind.
¹The Lord is my Shepherd, I shall not be in want. ²He makes me lie down in green pastures; He leads me beside quiet waters. ³He restores my soul.

Feeling a sense of peace, I retrieved my sketch pad and pencil from my car and began sketching what I saw and felt around me. After I finished, I examined what I had put on paper; there before me was a broken tree that had fallen across the river; it made a bridge. On the other side of the river were beautiful trees and lovely wild rose bushes, and on my side there was but a single rosebud with a tear-drop.

I saw myself and knew that in order to walk across that tree bridge to the other side where there was beauty and peace, I needed to seek help to be well again. Did I know then that God was at my side, and on my side? No, I was not aware of Him with me; not yet.

When I arrived in Redding, I checked myself into a mental health facility for a two-week stay. At last, I felt safe. The culmination of all the feelings I had sequestered over the years from the tragic losses I had experienced could no longer be contained. It was a pitiful time in my life; I was pitiful; yet my children, by then all grown and on their own, loved me unconditionally and supported and encouraged me. I was soon able to face the world again with a new resolve and a fresh start. I was able to accept my life and I would eventually come to love and embrace it; but right now, this would be my new normal.

Did God jump right in and take over, transforming me from that moment on? No, He didn't. I was still in the driver's seat and He was riding shotgun. He wasn't that obvious to me yet. I still saw Him as an unreachable force in the Heavens, and one to be reckoned with. If I gave Him too much thought, He frightened me; because I only knew Him to be a judging and distant God.

There were times I turned to Him in prayer, envisioning Him high above the earth somewhere in Heavenly places, not expecting Him to have time to listen. When I was young expectant mother, I prayed for healthy babies, and each and every one of them was healthy. I was grateful for that; but did not give Him thanks directly. I just didn't have that kind of relationship with Him. I prayed after Ken was killed; I was so broken I didn't know if He heard me or not; I didn't know Him that well. I prayed when my son Scott was dying; He answered that prayer; and I was grateful, but again, I did not give Him thanks; I didn't know Him that well. I prayed when my son Ronnie died; prayers of an anguished mother reaching up into a vast universe to an invisible, unreachable God, hoping He could hear me; I didn't realize a loving God was grieving with me; I didn't know Him that well.

So I guess I can say I have prayed off and on all my life. But I didn't know where my prayers went or if they were just floating around someplace in deep dark space.

Now, let me tell you how good God is! I had not gone to church on a regular basis since Ken died. So, I was surprised one day when on impulse I wanted a Bible, and then found myself in the religious section of a popular bookstore, browsing through different Bibles to see if there was one easier than another that I could read and understand. That day, in 1996, I found the Bible I would take home with me. Inexplicably, although in baby steps, my seeking had begun, and so too, my spiritual healing. I still had no clue what I was getting into, or where I was going, but I knew it wasn't going to be backward. I began to read a random chapter or verse every night before I went to bed. I had never read the Bible before, and most of it didn't make any sense to me; but I continued this ritual because I would feel a twinge of something missing if I didn't. Without my even realizing it at first, I began living a calmer and more peaceful life; the chaos that I had come to think of as normal, had all but disappeared! I had not taken my Bible reading at night as any sign of significant change in my life. It wasn't anything as obvious as Saul getting knocked off his horse, as the story is told in the Bible.

I was on my own, literally for the first time in my life, without a man to define me or children to rear. I wasn't responsible for anyone other than myself, and it felt good. I was experiencing joy in the solitude of my own company. Most people half my age had already discovered who they were, where they were headed, and were content with their life goals. I didn't care how far behind I was in discovering who I was — I knew how far I had come.

I relished my healthy state of mind. I had a great job that I loved, working at Mercy Medical Center, the hospital on the hill, dispatching helicopter and fixed-wing air and ground ambulances. I loved my job and my co-workers; we were a close-knit team and considered each other family.

Was this new outlook on my life my own doing? Well, at the time, I didn't give it that much thought. I was enjoying my life; that much I did know.

That year, I spent my first Christmas morning alone and I was feeling okay about it. I decorated my little apartment just as I did when I had a houseful of kids. I even bought myself a coat, wrapped it and put it under my tree. There wasn't an ounce of any "poor me" attitude, just contentment and well-being.

That New Year's happened to be the year I decided I wanted to stay home and not go out and party. I was good with that decision; a first for me. Now this is where it gets kind of out of character for me; I decided that it would be a nice thing to do, to randomly select five strangers, via AOL profile and just wish them a Happy Birthday. My thinking was that if they were home alone on this particular night, being New Years and their birthday, maybe a random birthday wish would cheer them. I felt it was a pretty safe thing to do, as I wasn't looking for a pen-pal and certainly not a relationship; it was more of a spontaneous idea that just seemed to bubble out of nowhere. (Is it a God thing, do you think? I still didn't know Him that well to even think that at the time.)

I chose five men that lived on the east coast; a safe 3,000 mile distance, so as not to encourage stalkers; and who were either, single, divorced or widowed. I arrived at that decision because I didn't want a parent to be alarmed if their child received a message from a stranger. I didn't send it to women because I didn't want them to be alarmed to receive a message from a woman they didn't know; and I didn't want to send it to married men for obvious reasons. So, to each of the five randomly selected men, I sent this note:

"You don't know me, but I just want to wish you a Happy Birthday.

Signed,
A perfect stranger."

I heard back from at least a couple of the recipients, thanking me for the birthday wishes, and as I read the responses, I smiled and then deleted their email. It was not my intent from the beginning to start a pen-pal email relationship. Mission accomplished. It felt good to do something random and kind for someone I didn't know while expecting nothing in return; a first for me.

It was about a week later, while at my computer, an AOL instant message window popped up on my screen. AOL was fairly new and I wasn't too familiar with the instant message aspect of it yet. But here was a message to me in real time! It said, "Just curious about the perfect stranger that commits random acts of kindness. I sell resort condominiums in Myrtle Beach, South Carolina. What do you do?"

As I read that short note, I was at once captivated. This man had a clever way with words that fascinated me, and I just had to respond that I dispatched fixed- and rotary-wing emergency air ambulances from Mercy Medical Center in Redding, California.

And so it was, we began what would become five thousand pages of email correspondence back and forth for the next twenty-two months. From January 1998 until about October the same year, it had been a wonderfully platonic relationship built on mutual trust and shared thoughts and experiences. We shared about the tragedies and triumphs we each had experienced. I found I could be totally honest with this man and didn't have to pretend to be anything but myself. He saw in me things I had never seen in myself; he was uplifting and encouraging to me. Here was a man who was far superior to me in intellect, education and who was worldly, interested in what I was thinking, doing and feeling and anxious to hear from me. He was interested in who I was, not what I could do for him. We had not exchanged pictures of each other, nor given any indication to the other about our looks or stature.

It was about October that I began to fancy him as sort of a prince charming and envisioned what it might be like to be with him. It was becoming a fantasy that just wasn't practical. That's when I began to pray to God, every night after reading my Bible; "God, if you have picked this man for me, let me know, or take this feeling away from me." I was so sincere in this prayer because I was content to be on my own now, and life seemed perfect in my world the way it was. Having anything other than a platonic email relationship would be ridiculous to contemplate, and would upset any shred of sensibility. "God," I prayed, "if this isn't pleasing to you, please take it from me."

It was December 5th, 1998, nearly one full year to the month that I sent that birthday greeting, he messaged me to ask if it was okay if he called me. It was a five-minute phone call. I fell in love with his accent. We made plans to meet, aware that others thought we were taking a risk that either of us may not be what we expected. However, we each knew the other more intimately than anyone else ever had because of our openness and honesty with one another. We knew we would be friends forever; that would not change. We met face-to-face for the first time on Valentine's Day weekend in 1999, and each felt instantly we were meant to be together; though we said nothing of the sort to each other just yet.

The ensuing months were a whirl-wind of activity with my flying to South Carolina to see his surroundings, and then his flying to California to meet my family. He was warned that he would be under their microscopic inspection at my request, because I didn't want to make any more major decisions without their input. I then flew to Georgia to meet his family. It was at the airport in Jacksonville, Florida on my trip back home that Ray got on one knee and proposed to me; that was September 5, 1999. I had been praying each night since October 1998 to take away any fantasies that I had of this prince charming if it wasn't meant to be. I wanted to be level headed and not lose all ground that I had gained. It felt so right! And indeed, it was.

We were married November 5, 1999 on the beach in Myrtle Beach, South Carolina, at sunset. Ray had bought a beautiful home for us just south of Myrtle Beach; we settled in and life was good. I was soon able to find work in Myrtle Beach, which was about a ten-mile commute. While on my commute, I would say a little prayer, like a Hail Mary or an Our Father. I don't know why, I just did; then it became a habit, just like my reading my Bible. I wasn't asking for anything, just touching base with God.

Life was wonderful, and Ray was everything I knew he would be. He was kind, loving, thoughtful, and encouraging every day; that's just who he was and is. I basked in his love and grew more confident in myself, that I was truly loveable just as I was. That I was capable of loving someone so deeply and perfectly was more than I had ever dreamed of. Wow, what a wonderful feeling!

At this point, my conversations to God were one-sided. I just felt the need to talk to him, not expecting Him to answer. I continued my routine of reading the Bible, though now I did it first thing in the morning before going to work; and then on my commute to work, I continued to say the prayers I had memorized as a child. Ray and I were kind of hit-and-miss on going to church on Sundays. He was raised Baptist and I was raised Catholic, so we decided to go to a non-denominational church. The one we tried seemed all about entertainment. That didn't work for us at all. Every now and then I went to church with a friend from work; but going to church on a regular basis was not yet part of my routine.

Life was about to take a different direction in 2001. We made a joint decision that we needed to move to Ocilla, Georgia to be close to Ray's elderly mother. Ray was an only child and his mother was well into her eighties trying to look after herself, as well as her nearly-invalid sister. It was time to make a big change. Ray was concerned that my being from a good-sized town in California, I might have a problem adjusting to the much slower pace of a small Southern town. He had genuine angst over it. I did not. My thought was, I will be who I am, and that's all I can be. It was September 11th, 2001 when we took a huge step into uncertainty, selling our beautiful home, leaving our stable, good paying jobs, to move to a small-town community with a population of about 3,000 that offered few jobs and fewer places to rent. But the one thing we knew we had was each other, and we were doing the right thing for the right reason. We knew it would all work out.

We found a small and very modest little house on a huge lot for very cheap rent. The amazing thing about this little place was the yard. The house itself and every tree on the lot was surrounded by azalea bushes, and when they bloomed the beauty of it all just took my breath away. I remember emailing my Aunt Elynor in California, showing her a picture of the yard and telling her that I felt in my heart, I was exactly where I needed to be. I had no idea how profound that statement was.

Isaiah 45:5 NIV
⁵ I am the LORD, and there is no other;
apart from me there is no God.
I will strengthen you,
though you have not acknowledged me.

PART 7

Saved by Grace, Through Faith

Chapter One

BORN AGAIN

R ay and I settled into our new life in Ocilla like hand in glove. The fit was perfect in this charming Southern town. Ray got reacquainted with old friends and former classmates, having grown up here, and his friends quickly became my friends. Where I came from in California, I was basically an anonymous figure outside of my close circle of friends; but, I soon learned, the South was different. I found that everybody was either related or connected to one another in some way, and everybody pretty much knew what everyone else was doing.

In a small Southern town like Ocilla, it would be impossible for me to remain anonymous; people would be curious about who I was and where I came from. I had no lineage that could be connected to an introduction, such as, "her daddy owned the cotton gin," or "her granddaddy was the sheriff," or "her family had the movie theater where the grocery store is now," and so on and so forth. I loved it; the charm of

Southern women and the courtesy of Southern gentlemen was a whole new world for me.

What I also discovered was that nearly everyone went to church on Sunday! I thought it would be a good idea to start going to church, so Ray and I set out to find one that would fit both of our needs. I, being raised Catholic and Ray, a former Deacon in the Baptist church, decided we would need to make a compromise if we wanted to attend church together. We attended a few different churches and finally settled on one. For the first time since my elementary school days, I began attending church on a regular basis.

I also began attending a Sunday school for the first time and discovered I loved it. In the beginning, I was shy about speaking up, embarrassed that I didn't know my way around the Bible and had never spontaneously prayed out loud in public. It was a great learning experience. The women in my Sunday school class became close Christian friends. I realized I was beginning to evolve into a gentler, kinder and more patient kind of person.

It was as if the slate had been wiped clean from the life I lived in California. However, when some of my newfound friends would mention in passing that so and so had been married three or four times, they would all seem to gasp at the news. I wondered what they would think of me if they knew how many times I had been married. I was the *woman at the well*! There was a part of me that felt as if I had this secret and that if anyone "really knew me" they would think of me a lot differently. At this point in my Christian journey

I wasn't ready to share everything about me. Instinct told me it would not benefit anyone, and would just be used as fodder for gossip. I wasn't going to lie if someone should ask; but I was fairly certain that Southern manners would prevent that question from ever being asked of me.

Ray and I finally moved from our modest little rental house into our own home right on the main street in town. It was our dream home. In the house between the kitchen and the formal dining room was an enclosed breakfast room with a butler's pantry; I immediately claimed it for my private study. It was there I found solitude and the perfect place to read my Bible in the morning. It became my sanctuary, a place to pray in private without distractions, to meditate and to find inspiration. Some may see it as just a quaint little breakfast nook with a small desk, but to me it has become sacred.

So what was going on with me spiritually? I definitely wasn't the same person that moved to South Carolina in 1999. Was it the South? Was it the Southern hospitality? Was it praying every day and reading my Bible? Was it going to church every Sunday? I was not yet able to put my finger on it. When I lived in California, I didn't mind letting loose with a swear word now and then; in fact when I worked at the police department, it became second nature to me. But in the South, where I had now been planted and was now blooming, people just didn't talk like that; I was able to get rid of that very bad habit almost effortlessly.

Until our church did a study on "Purpose Driven Life," by Rick Warren, I had no clue that I was here on earth for a specific purpose. But, after that, I was convinced that I did have a purpose, and I was eager to find out what that purpose was. The sands of time were rapidly filling the bottom of the hourglass and I was concerned that I might miss out on finding my purpose altogether.

One Sunday, the pastor invited a church member to come to the pulpit and share the weekend experience she had just had on a Christian retreat called Walk to Emmaus. I had never heard of it before; but when she got through sharing, I knew I wanted to experience what she did. I found a sponsor and turned in my application, and then waited and waited and waited. Eventually, I figured that I just wouldn't be chosen to go. It was approximately eighteen months later that the subject was brought up again in church, and they were asking if men wanted to attend the Walk to Emmaus. Ray raised his hand. He was given a sponsor, and completed an application, and within a couple of weeks he was on his way to what they referred to as the men's fall Walk to Emmaus. I was told at the same time that I would be attending a couple of weeks after he completed his weekend.

Ray left on a Thursday afternoon. When he returned on Sunday evening, he was wearing all kinds of necklaces and stuff pinned to his shirt and was grinning like I had never seen before. This was so not like him! I couldn't imagine what had occurred over those past few days that transformed this man I thought I knew so well. I couldn't explain it but he was different, in a most remarkable way.

Soon after, it was my turn to go on the women's weekend Walk to Emmaus. Just as Ray, I also left on a Thursday afternoon, not knowing what my experience would be like. I was hoping I would learn more about God, and maybe find out what purpose He had for me in this life. By Friday night I was afraid I wasn't going to find out what my purpose was. I was ready to give up before I failed or was rejected by God. Maybe I didn't belong at this retreat, because it seemed a lot of the women were much more advanced spiritually than I. I stayed off to myself during break time because I really felt out of my comfort zone. The pastor of my church was on the spiritual team for the week-end, and seeing me alone, obviously nervous and distressed, he reached out to me. He said he understood how I was feeling, it was natural; but he thought I was over-anticipating and for me to just relax, "put it in neutral" and I would see that things would get better each passing hour. I promised I would try that.

By the end of that weekend I discovered I could have a personal relationship with Jesus! I didn't know it then, but from that moment on, I would never be the same. My life had a brand new meaning. I then understood the grin on Ray's face when he came home from his weekend. There was nothing magical about that weekend retreat, but there was definitely an awakening of the spirit within me; the Holy Spirit. I wanted more of Jesus. I wanted to do more, in His name. His presence in my life was made known to me in my spirit.

I began to look back over my life, now seeing with different eyes, where He had been with me all the time. I began seeking Him in earnest, reading devotionals and stories about Christianity. And, as my life became less about me and more about Him, one morning in the quiet of my study, I got on my face on the floor and with sobs of gratitude, I accepted Jesus Christ as my Savior, and that day I gave my life to Him; not just a piece of me, nor half of me, but all of me. I was His to do with as He willed. I would learn to put my trust completely in Him, and less in people or things. It was then that I understood "Born again!"

He had patiently been waiting on me for this day. He knew it would come; He had been preparing me. He took His time and taught me patience.

He uses different circumstances for different people. For some, like Paul in the Bible, His method is instant and dramatic. For others, like me, it is more subtle. It took years of suffering and working through selfishness and self-pity, the opportunity to meet and marry my soul mate, of praying to a God I didn't understand but knew existed, all circumstances that weren't by chance but were part of His perfect plan, for me to finally accept His gift of Salvation.

My life is no worse nor better than anyone else's; tis neither fairytale nor extraordinary nor without its peaks and valleys; but my life in Christ is what makes it worth it! I have in me a joy that can't be taken from me, for its source comes from the joy of the Lord in me!

I delight in bringing His message to others as a volunteer on the Walk to Emmaus. It is one of the tools God used to open my eyes to Him; a weekend that changed me in a very profound way.

Another of God's tools He uses, and one that is dear to my heart, is the Kairos ministry. It is very similar to Emmaus, but ministered to men and women behind prison walls. Being part of that ministry as a volunteer for the women, gave me a totally different outlook on societies' lowest of the low. To witness God's saving grace for those who feel worthless and hopeless and unworthy, whom society has cast aside, is nothing short of amazing. Yes, God's amazing grace transforms these women who are sinners, just as I, from a life of hopelessness to one of joy. For many of them, it is the very first time they experience unconditional love.

That God would use me to bring His message to others is a blessing of joy to my heart! Finding things to do to help others, takes the attention off oneself and onto others. I think that's how God intends for us to be. Looking to reach out in the smallest of ways may be a major help to another. The Lord has chosen to use me, not in any big way, but in a lot of small ways, and as I become more obedient to His whispers, and the more I give of myself, it seems the more "My cup runneth over."

PART 8

Forgiveness

Chapter One

FORGIVEN AND FORGIVING

❦

Of all the chapters in my life, being forgiven and forgiving have been the greatest of all blessings. First, I had to learn to forgive myself. Once God forgave me, there was no reason for me to hang on to my own un-forgiveness. Then, after reciting the Lord's Prayer for all of my life, one day it dawned on me what it meant when I prayed, *"forgive us our trespasses as we forgive those who trespass against us..."* Wow! Did I really want God to forgive me only as much as I forgave others? I should hope not! I found that if I told God that I <u>wanted</u> to forgive someone, but it just wasn't in my heart to actually forgive and let go of bitterness, that He would soon soften my heart to release the bitterness and give me the grace to forgive. What a great feeling it is to forgive and be forgiven. And so it is that I wrote the following about the forgiveness of the men responsible for the death of Ken, my first love and father of five of my children.

Chapter Two

I FORGIVE YOU

⁜

I remember reading in the paper shortly after Ken's was killed, that the police had arrested three suspects in his shooting death. All three were not much younger than I, maybe a year or two. I had decided I didn't want to go to their trial and re-live that tragic night. My brothers Jim and Joe were in agreement with me, thinking that would not be healthy for me nor the baby I was carrying within me; they said they would go in my place and report back to me what they felt I needed to know. I was satisfied with that arrangement.

These three young men were drug addicts needing money to feed their addiction. They apparently observed Ken as manager and waited for all the other employees to leave. I am guessing they must have come in through the back door as Ken was getting ready to leave with the bank deposits; I am not clear on the part of how they got in. They testified in court that they had no intention of shooting him;

they said that Ken was being cooperative and there wasn't any reason to shoot; the gun they brought in with them was only meant to scare him into giving them the money. The defense attorney offered that the defendants didn't realize the gun had a hair trigger and that it fired accidently. They pled not guilty to first degree murder. They were found guilty of second degree murder and sentenced to life in prison with the possibility of parole after seven years.

I held no animosity toward them. In fact for several years I had no feelings toward them one way or the other. They were young, foolish and they were addicts that needed a fix. My husband was at the wrong place at the wrong time. My being angry or hostile would not change one thing. I didn't really know why I couldn't muster up anger and bitterness for what they did, but I have figured out since then, that God had a hand in that. I had forgotten about the reoccurring dreams I had when Ken and I first married; but thinking back, it may very well have been preparing me for this time in my life. I can think of no other earthly reason to have experienced them.

I didn't forgive these guys, because truthfully, I never gave it a thought about whether I should or shouldn't. As years went by though, I would occasionally think about them and wonder if they got out of prison; if they changed their lives; if taking a man's life had any impact on their lives. And then, I would go into what I now call, survival mode and put it out of my mind.

As I write, it has been forty-five years since Ken's death and only within the past year have I become curious about the men who took his life; enough so that I would like to find a way to contact them and tell them I have forgiven them. Whether they want forgiveness, or whether they accept forgiveness, is between God and them. I know, for me personally, that being forgiven is life changing.

God has forgiven me, and although my sins may look different than their sins to this earthly world, my sins are no less despicable in God's eyes, than theirs. God lifted my burden of sin and guilt, and set me free. I want the same for those three men; that they have the opportunity to be set free from the bondage of sin and guilt; I pray that for them. And, I pray, if it is God's will, that I might meet them one day and let them know I have forgiven them in my heart and have asked God to forgive them also.

Romans 4:7-8 NIV
⁷Blessed are they whose transgressions are forgiven, whose sins are covered.
⁸Blessed is the man whose sin the Lord will never count against him.

I will always miss Ken; he was the spiritual leader in our home, and I know where he is. His work was completed on earth according to God's perfect plan. I walked through the fires of hell on earth, partly of my own making, because I relied on myself and not God. After all these many years, I finally get it! I have come to the place in my Christian journey where I can now fully proclaim my belief in the risen Lord and profess that Jesus is my Savior. I give God all the glory for all He has done in me; for it is by grace alone, through faith, that I am saved.

1Corinthians 15: 54-57 NIV
[54]....."Death has been swallowed up in victory."
[55]"Where, O death, is your victory?
Where, O death is your sting?"
[56]The sting of death is sin, and the power of sin is the law.
[57]But thanks be to God! He gives us the victory through our Lord Jesus Christ.

PART 9

What Now?

Chapter One

THE GIFT OF GRACE – YOURS FOR THE ASKING

My Christian journey continues each day, now and forever. It is in the quietness of my study that I go each morning expecting God to make His presence known, and He never fails me. Some mornings I will write in my journal, and then just be still in His presence; other mornings I will do all the talking, checking off of my laundry list of wants and needs, and asking Him to take care of it for me. I keep Him on my lips throughout the day by thanking Him for even the smallest of things, whether it be a trip on the rug that didn't result in a fall, a lost item found, or puffy white clouds that dance across the sky changing from images of angels into little lambs, or the gift of good health; I just say, "Thank you Jesus."

I share my story to give hope to those who have lost hope or have very little, not because of anything I have done, but because of what He has done in me.

If you are carrying the burdens of shame, guilt, unworthiness, bitterness, and/or unforgiveness in your heart, did you realize you leave no room for Jesus? He has a gift for you; go to Him in prayer, just as you are, and prepare to receive the gift of grace! Christ has already fought our battle and is victorious over sin once and for all. Step out in faith and lay your burdens down at the foot of the cross and leave them there; He will give you peace and joy that transcends all understanding.

Philippians 4:6-7 NIV
[6] Do not be anxious about anything, but in every situation, by prayer and petition, with thanksgiving, present your requests to God. [7] And the peace of God, which transcends all understanding, will guard your hearts and your minds in Christ Jesus.

It gives me great joy to remind you that you are precious sons and daughters of the most-high King, and heir to royalty in the Kingdom of God. It is my prayer that He gives you ears to hear His slightest whispers; and eyes to see the needs of others before yourself; may He give you knowledge, wisdom, courage and boldness to speak of His mercy and goodness and proclaim the Good News. And may He also bless your life abundantly.

Ephesians 2:8-10 NIV
For it is by grace you have been saved, through faith–and this is not from yourself, it is the gift of God-[9]not by works, so

that no one can boast. [10]For we are God's workmanship, created in Christ Jesus to do good works, which God prepared in advance for us to do.

EPILOGUE

I want to share with you an excerpt from a devotional I read each morning. It comes from a book by Sarah Young, titled, *Jesus Calling – Enjoying Peace in His Presence,* taken from the July fourteenth devotion:

Keep walking with Me along the path I have chosen for you. Your desire to live close to Me is a delight to My heart... Together we will forge a pathway up the high mountain...

The new Mr. and Mrs. Raymond L. Mann, Jr.

November 5, 1999

ENDNOTES

Prologue; Oswald Chambers, My Utmost for His Highest. Daily Devotional November 5th. (Copyright info: this edition by special arrangement and permission of discovery House Publishers. Copyright ©1935 by Dodd, Mead and Company, Inc. Copyright renewed 1963 by Oswald Chambers Publications Association, Ltd.)

Jesus is Lord of All; Lyrics by William J. Gaither and Gloria Gaither © 1973 Gaither Music Company (admin. By Gaither Copyright Mgmt.) All rights reserved.

Epilogue; Sarah Young, "Jesus Calling – Enjoying Peace in His Presence" A 365 Day Devotional. Excerpt taken from July fourteenth devotion. © 2004 Sarah Young. Published in Nashville, Tennessee by Thomas Nelson. Thomas Nelson is a registered trademark of Thomas Nelson, Inc. For information, please e-mail SpecialMarkets@ThomasNelson.com

Back Cover; Quotation in italics is from Hamlet, Act 3, Scene 1, by Shakespeare; taken from online source; http://poetry.rapgenius.com/William-shakespeare-hamlet-act-3-scene-1-lyrics#note-1102513

—

CPSIA information can be obtained at www.ICGtesting.com
Printed in the USA
LVOW13s0044280813

349795LV00002B/4/P